The Mental Health and Wellbeing Workout for Teens

of related interest

My Anxiety Handbook
Getting Back on Track
Sue Knowles, Bridie Gallagher and Phoebe McEwen
Illustrated by Emmeline Pidgen
ISBN 978 1 78592 440 8
eISBN 978 1 78450 813 5

Starving the Anxiety Gremlin
A Cognitive Behavioural Therapy Workbook on
Anxiety Management for Young People
Kate Collins-Donnelly
ISBN 978 1 84905 341 9
eISBN 978 0 85700 673 8

Banish Your Body Image Thief
A Cognitive Behavioural Therapy Workbook on
Building Positive Body Image for Young People
Kate Collins-Donnelly
ISBN 978 1 84905 463 8
eISBN 978 0 85700 842 8

Banish Your Self-Esteem Thief
A Cognitive Behavioural Therapy Workbook on
Building Positive Self-Esteem for Young People
Kate Collins-Donnelly
ISBN 978 1 84905 462 1
eISBN 978 0 85700 841 1

Teen Anxiety
A CBT and ACT Activity Resource Book
for Helping Anxious Adolescents
Raychelle Cassada Lohmann
ISBN 978 1 84905 969 5
eISBN 978 0 85700 859 6

Starving the Exam Stress Gremlin
A Cognitive Behavioural Therapy Workbook on
Managing Exam Stress for Young People
Kate Collins-Donnelly
ISBN 978 1 84905 698 4
eISBN 978 1 78450 214 0

THE MENTAL HEALTH AND WELLBEING WORKOUT FOR TEENS

Skills and Exercises from ACT and CBT for Healthy Thinking

Paula Nagel

Illustrated by Gary Bainbridge

Jessica Kingsley *Publishers*
London and Philadelphia

First published in 2019
by Jessica Kingsley Publishers
73 Collier Street
London N1 9BE, UK
and
400 Market Street, Suite 400
Philadelphia, PA 19106, USA

www.jkp.com

Copyright © Paula Nagel 2019
Illustrations copyright © Gary Bainbridge 2019

Library of Congress Cataloging in Publication Data
Names: Nagel, Paula (Educational psychologist), author.
Title: The mental health and wellbeing workout for teens : skills and
    exercises from ACT and CBT for healthy thinking / Paula Nagel.
Description: London ; Philadelphia : Jessica Kingsley Publishers, 2019. |
    Audience: Age 12-18. | Includes bibliographical references and index.
Identifiers: LCCN 2018030534 | ISBN 9781785923944 (alk. paper)
Subjects: LCSH: Health behavior in adolescence. | Teenagers--Health and
    hygiene. | Acceptance and commitment therapy--Problems, exercises, etc. |
    Cognitive therapy for teenagers--Problems exercises, etc.
Classification: LCC RJ47.53 .N34 2019 | DDC 613/.0433--dc23 LC
record available at https://lccn.loc.gov/2018030534

British Library Cataloguing in Publication Data
A CIP catalogue record for this book is available from the British Library

ISBN 978 1 78592 394 4
eISBN 978 1 78450 753 4

Printed and bound in Great Britain

MIX
Paper from
responsible sources
FSC® C013056

CONTENTS

INTRODUCTION
WELCOME TO THE MENTAL HEALTH AND WELLBEING WORKOUT

I wonder what you were thinking when you opened this book?

Workout? For mental health? What's that about? Is it like going to the gym for your brain?

I've seen some things on social media about stress and depression. That's mental health, right? Is that what this book is about?

I've been feeling a bit 'off' lately...I wonder if there's anything in here that might help me feel more like me again?

Nice cover – let's see what's inside...

I'm pretty bored...I've got nothing better to do right now, so I might as well have a flick through.

While some of you will be aware of the thoughts that led you to pick up this book, many of you won't have registered them at all:

> Actually...I'm not really sure what I was thinking...

> ????

> I don't know if I was thinking anything...

And that's totally normal. We have so many thoughts running through our minds that it would be impossible to keep track of them all…and nor would we want to. Imagine if you had to consciously think about every single decision you made…like whether to scratch that itch on your nose with your forefinger or little finger, how to place one foot in front of the other when you walk to the fridge for a drink, or having to plan your route to school or college every time you leave the house. You'd have no space left in your mind to do anything other than the thinking needed to keep your body working, and to do the routine stuff to get you through the day. And I'm guessing you've got so many other things you'd rather be thinking about…

But there's a lot going on in our minds, whether we're aware of it or not. Some people believe that we have around 40 thoughts a minute. That's nearly two-and-a-half thousand thoughts an hour! Of course we don't notice most of them. Many will be ones we've had before, so they may be automatic, a bit like a habit. Some of these automatic, thinking habits will be helpful ones that allow us to get things done quickly with minimum effort, motivate and make us feel good about ourselves, and help us find ways to solve problems. But other thinking habits will be less helpful and might actually stop us doing what we want to do, or being how we'd like to be.

This Mental Health and Wellbeing Workout will help you get to know your thinking habits a little better, especially those unhelpful, automatic thinking habits that can get in the way, and the Workout Team will help us to do this. So before we go any further, let's meet the Workout Team…

It's time for me to make a confession. I was teenager a long time ago and although I think I can remember that time quite well, the world is a very different place now. So while writing this book I talked to a number of teenagers and young people, and I've drawn on their ideas and stories, as well as the ideas of those I've had the privilege to work with over the years. So I hope the examples and illustrations feel real and relevant to you. Of course I've made changes here and there to keep the stories and comments anonymous, and I haven't included any real names…but Workout Team, you know who you are! Thank you!

What is mental health?

Many people, including adults, still feel uneasy about the phrase 'mental health' – although we hear and talk about mental health more than ever before, there's still a stigma attached to it. The Workout Team shared some of the things they have heard others say about the words 'mental health':

…fruit loop…

…crazy…

…psycho…

…mad…

…la-la…

…not right in the head…

As well as being inappropriate, these phrases have another thing in common – they link mental health to mental illness. But we all have mental health, just like we all have physical health. And in the same way that our physical health will be in good shape and not-so-good shape, so will our mental health.

Let's think for a moment about our physical health, so we can understand more about our mental health too.

We don't think twice about talking about what we do…or don't do…to keep physically fit and in shape. And we usually don't mind talking about feeling under the weather because of a cold or a cough or a sore throat. And we certainly wouldn't call someone a cruel name if they had broken their leg or sprained a muscle, would we? So why do we think our mental health is any different? Our mental health will have its ups and downs, just like our physical health. Some days we might feel mentally robust, that we can face whatever comes our way, manage to get through things and stay mentally strong throughout. But having good mental health doesn't mean we will be happy and positive every single minute of every single day. People with good mental health will have good days and bad days. However, someone with good mental health will be more likely to think of things they can do to get through the bad days without it affecting them in the long term.

Our physical and mental health are both part of our general wellbeing and are so connected that sometimes they're hard to separate. For example, big feelings like stress, anxiety, anger or sadness have an impact on our physical health too, and can make us feel in physical pain or more prone to bugs and infection. Physical and mental health are both part of our general health and fitness.

What the Mental Health and Wellbeing Workout is about

There are some exercises in this book to help you get to know your thinking habits and to find ways of managing them. Many of them have taken ideas from Cognitive Behavioural Therapy (CBT) and Acceptance and Commitment Therapy (ACT). These two psychological approaches have some things in common but some differences too. Both of them stress the importance of being aware of our thoughts and how they can affect how we feel and what we do, but they differ in their approaches to managing unhelpful thinking.

CBT looks at the link between our thoughts, feelings and actions, and how unhelpful thinking can impact on how we feel and how we behave.

It often looks at ways of challenging and changing unhelpful thoughts in order to change behaviour. CBT has a strong research base and is often the recommended approach for working with a range of emotional and behavioural problems such as depression and anxiety.

ACT is a newer psychological therapy and builds on some CBT approaches. However, rather than focusing on challenging and changing thoughts, ACT explores how responding differently to unhelpful thoughts can help manage them. So, as it says in the title, part of ACT is accepting that unhelpful thoughts happen, learning to live with them, and responding to them more flexibly. ACT incorporates many ideas from mindfulness, which focuses on directing attention to the here and now and noticing what is happening in the present moment.

A vital step for both approaches is recognising unhelpful thoughts in the first place, so this book will give you ideas for noticing your thoughts as well as accepting and responding more flexibly to them, and challenging and changing them. These ideas are reflected in three types of exercises included in this book:

→ **Warming Up exercises** – to help you notice and get to know your thoughts. After all, we need to recognise our thoughts before we can do anything with them!

→ **Stretch and Flex-ercises** – to develop greater awareness and acceptance, and promote flexible thinking. Having flexible muscles can help your body cope with stresses and strains. In the same way, thinking flexibly and finding different ways to respond to your thoughts can help you cope with the ups and downs in life.

→ **Think-ercises** – to help you build mental strength to respond differently to the thoughts and, in some cases, change their shape… just like when you strengthen a muscle!

Like any good workout, it's beneficial to include a range of different exercises. Try to mix and match the exercises and find the ones that suit you best – that way you'll be more likely to stick to them!

It is important to take care of your thoughts, as they are a big part of your mental health, and these exercises can help keep your thoughts fit and healthy. Left unchecked, unhelpful thinking habits can have a negative impact on mental health.

Here's what the Workout Team said about mental health:

We all have it…it's not a choice.

We should talk about it more so we don't think of being mentally ill when we hear the words 'mental health'.

We need to learn how to look after our minds just like we look after our bodies.

This book focuses on looking after your thoughts to keep you mentally fit and well. *But other things can affect your mental health and wellbeing too.*

Here's what the Workout Team said about the things that can affect their mental health:

Stuff that happens in life. Sometimes it's the big things that happen, like someone dying, breaking up with someone, or having a big fight with a friend. And sometimes it's the things you have to do that get too much. Things like exams, and homework and interviews.

It doesn't have to be the big things either. Lots of things in life can affect how mentally strong you feel – it could be something you see on the news or read about, falling out with a friend, moving house. Sometimes even the things that are sort of nice and that you look forward to, like starting a new job or school, can make you feel stressed at the same time.

Feeling physically ill and unwell makes me feel like I can't cope anymore.

Not having the right amount to eat, drink or sleep can make me moody or grumpy.

When these things happen it's worth being extra aware of your thoughts, as unhelpful thinking habits can make things feel even worse.

At times like this it's also worth thinking about the things that can help you stay mentally fit and well. These things will be different for different people, but here are some ideas from the Workout Team:

Hanging out with my mates.

Doing my favourite things – for me that's curling up with a gossipy magazine and my headphones in, but my best friend likes to take her dog for a run when she feels low.

Just being around other people and being able to do things for them even when I'm feeling rubbish. It makes me forget about stuff for a while. Even if it's just doing something small like holding open a door. Sounds stupid but it makes me feel better…

Trying to get enough rest and doing things that relax me – like having a duvet day with a hot chocolate and a good film.

Catching up on my sleep.

Having my favourite comfort food.

Although this book will help you to plan a personal workout to notice and manage your unhelpful thinking habits, it's also important to consider what else you can do to help your wellbeing. Think of it like going to the gym for a physical workout – your body is likely to benefit even more from physical exercise when you do other things too. Things like…

→ Getting enough sleep.

→ Having a good diet and putting a piece of fruit or an energy bar and drink in your gym bag.

→ Exercising with a friend.

→ Listening to music while you exercise.

→ Targeting areas where you want to be stronger.

→ Varying your exercise…not doing the same things all of the time.

So what will you put in your 'mental health gym bag' to get the most from your Mental Health and Wellbeing Workout? Here are some ideas…

→ Doing things I'm good at and enjoy.

→ Spending time with friends.

➜ Being physically active.

➜ Getting enough sleep and rest.

➜ Helping others.

➜ Eating well – not too much or too little.

Can you think of anything else?

An overview

The chapters that follow in Part 1 will give you an idea of the psychology behind the workout, explain the thinking behind some of the ideas, and introduce you to some of the exercises. Part 2 is designed for you to dip in and out of, and focuses on different kinds of unhelpful thinking habits. Throughout the book you'll be encouraged to keep a note of your thoughts. You might want to keep a workout notebook so you can keep all of your ideas together, or perhaps keep them in the notes on your phone.

There are three chapters in Part 1. In Chapter 1, we explore helpful and unhelpful thinking habits, examples of what they might look like and when they might happen. We invite you to get to know your helpful and unhelpful thoughts a little better with some easy-to-do **Warming Up exercises**.

In Chapter 2 we look at unhelpful thoughts in action by taking us through Marc's miserable morning. We see how Marc's unhelpful thinking habits quickly take hold, affecting how he feels and what he does. We introduce the different exercises, and illustrate how they could help Marc to manage his thoughts differently.

The **Stretch and Flex-ercises** in Chapter 3 will give you some ideas for noticing and thinking flexibly about your unhelpful thinking habits so that they bother you less. If you stick with the exercises you'll probably find you're better able to recognise and accept your unhelpful thoughts, and you'll begin to respond to them in different ways. Try to do something from the **Stretch and Flex-ercises** every day.

In Part 2, we share some common unhelpful thinking habits that most of us will experience from time to time. If you recognise any of the unhelpful thoughts in your own thinking, take a look at the **Think-ercises** at the end of each chapter. If you'd like to change the shape of these unhelpful thoughts, try out some of the exercises and choose the ones that feel right for you. The **Think-ercises** can be carried out alongside the **Warming Up exercises** and **Stretch and Flex-ercises**.

Although each chapter looks at a different kind of thinking habit, in real life unhelpful thoughts often stick together and work in gangs. So it's okay if you notice a few unhelpful thoughts at the same time. Similarly, although the **Think-ercises** at the end of each chapter are linked to a particular unhelpful thought, it's a good idea to mix and match ideas and exercises from the different chapters.

Here's an overview of the different kinds of unhelpful thoughts covered in Part 2:

→ Social comparison (aka the self-hater): falling into the habit of comparing yourself to others in an unhelpful, negative way.

→ Catastrophising (aka but what if…): over-estimating the likelihood of something bad happening and under-estimating your ability to cope.

→ Black-and-white thinking (aka all-or-nothing thinking): thinking about things in extremes and forgetting to consider the range of possibilities in between.

→ Negative filtering (aka looking through gloomy goggles): dismissing and discounting the positives in favour of a negative way of looking at things.

→ Perfectionism (aka Unreal Ideal): when striving for perfection becomes more about a fear of failure than doing your very best.

→ Personalisation (aka Over-Owning It): thinking you're to blame for everything.

→ Mind Reading (aka Filling in the Blanks): when second-guessing other people's motives gets in the way.

→ Emotional Reasoning (aka Feelings Rule, Okay!): when feelings take over and you believe that if you feel it, then it must be true.

In the final chapter, Chapter 9, we think about the things that matter to you, and how you can make the most of your unique skills and attributes to keep sight of the life you really want to lead.

Part 1

Part 2

HELPFUL AND UNHELPFUL THINKING

(AKA BEST FRIEND AND FRENEMY THOUGHTS)

Everyone knows it can be hard to kick a habit, and that applies to thinking habits too, especially as it can be hard to notice unhelpful thinking habits in the first place. Thinking habits can be so ingrained that they become a part of you, and something you're not really aware of.

So what?

Right now you might be thinking, 'So what? If I don't notice what I'm thinking, why does it matter? And why on earth would I want to change something I'm not even aware of? I'll leave my thoughts well alone… thank you very much…'

But you might want to think again. Because even when we're not aware of them, our thoughts play an important role in how we feel and what we do.

Read through the following statements and see if any ring true for you. And if they do, make a note of them. Perhaps try thinking about how often they happen. Take a rough guess and mark each statement according to how regularly you behave or feel that way. If it happens only sometimes, for example a few times a month, write 's'; if it is more likely to happen weekly, mark it with a 'w'; if it's something that feels quite familiar to you, perhaps happening most days, then mark it with an 'f'. Once you've ticked the boxes, count the number of 'w's' and 'f's' you've noted. If you find that you're usually noticing these kinds of statements on a weekly or daily basis, it might be a sign that your unhelpful thinking habits are taking over:

1. Do you ever feel hijacked by your emotions? Do big feelings – such as sadness, fear, shame, guilt, worry, anger – creep up on you out of nowhere and quickly take over?

2. Do you ever find yourself saying or thinking that everyone's got it much easier than you, or that others don't have the right to treat you how they do?

3. Do you ever say or do things that you really regret afterwards? Do you find yourself wishing you'd been able to push a pause button before you reacted?

4. Do you worry so much about what others think or say about you that it sometimes stops you from speaking up or being how you really want to be?

5. Do you ever re-play what you have said or done, over and over, in your head for hours…or even days afterwards?

6. Are you easily wound up? Do you see 'red' and lose your temper at the flick of a switch?

7. Do you try to find ways of pushing away or avoiding the difficult feelings?

8. Do you ever think that people are trying to make a fool of you or show you up?

9. Do you try to ignore strong feelings by distracting yourself? Are some of the things you do to avoid those feelings bad for you, like eating or drinking too much, or hurting yourself?

10. Do you ever think, 'Why me?' and that life just isn't fair?

We're only human after all...

Probably *all* of us will be able to answer 'yes' to some of these statements at different times in our lives. And that's entirely normal. We're all human beings trying to get through life in the best way we can. That includes coping with a range of situations, good and not so good, and dealing with a variety of people, nice and not so nice. And we won't always manage the difficult times or the difficult people in the most helpful way. We're only human after all! But if you can spot behaviours like the ones in the statements above on a regular basis, then it can become a problem...and unhelpful thinking habits are likely to be part of that problem.

If you've ticked a few of those statements, it might be a sign that your unhelpful thinking habits are taking over. Please keep on reading, because this book will help you get to know your unhelpful thinking habits so you can decide how to manage them before they take total control.

A few things about unhelpful thoughts...

Before we go any further, let's get a few things out in the open about unhelpful or 'frenemy' thoughts.

They don't like the here and now

Unhelpful thoughts don't like the here and now; they much prefer to ponder on the past or stress about the future. So when we're lost in thought, or mind-wandering, our frenemy thoughts tend to take us back to the things we've already said or done, or to the things that haven't yet happened...and not usually in a good way!

People who've studied mind-wandering say that most of us automatically drift into the past or the future when we're thinking, and that we aren't usually having helpful thoughts when we do so. When we think about the past, we tend to think about things we wish we'd done differently and give ourselves a hard time about it. And when we think of the future, we tend to worry and stress about what might happen.

Here's what the Workout Team said about their mind-wandering thoughts. They shared some of the typical thoughts that pulled them back to the past:

> Why did I say that to him? What was I thinking? And what must he think of me now?

> I should have told her what I really think instead of smiling like an idiot...why didn't I do that? I'm such a pushover. I really hate myself sometimes.

And the thoughts that propelled them into the future:

> What if I forget what I'm supposed to say? I'll look stupid, and everyone will know I'm a fake.

> I don't want to go to the party...I don't really know anyone else who's going, and I'll end up sitting on my own. I've never liked parties anyway. I'm going to say I'm busy.

The Workout Team noticed how their mind wandering thoughts were often linked to difficult, unpleasant feelings, things like feeling stupid or not good enough, or ashamed of things that had already happened, worrying about what other people were thinking or saying, and stressing about what might happen in the future.

What's more, the Workout Team noticed that they weren't usually aware when their thoughts were drifting to the past or the future. It wasn't something they were choosing to think about…it just seemed to happen automatically, like a bad habit. Before they knew it, frenemy thoughts dragged them away from the here and now, into the past or the future.

Mind-wandering's not all bad, though. There's nothing wrong in think-ing about what has happened or what lies ahead. It can be a good thing. In fact, it can be extremely helpful to run things through your mind to help you come up with new solutions to problems, understand things better, and get creative. Being lost in thought can also be calming and relaxing, especially when you think about things, people or places you find pleasant and enjoyable. But mind-wandering is most helpful when you're aware of what you're doing and when it is your choice to think about those things in that moment. The problem is that frenemy thinking tends to take over when we're mind-wandering, pulling us into the past or propelling us into to the future before we've even noticed.

So if you find you're going over and over things in your mind without realising until it's too late, then you might be letting frenemy thoughts control you. And you might end up stuck in the past or fearing the future.

The next time you find yourself thinking about something in the past or the future, try to notice if it's something you actually *want* to think about. Did you really want to go there again? Was it your choice? Or did you find yourself thinking about these things before you even realised?

Ask yourself who's in control – you or your thoughts?

Which takes us to our second point.

They're control freaks

Frenemy thoughts work best when they're in control, and they gain that control by sneaking up and taking over all of your headspace before you realise what's happening. Before you know it you're thinking yet again of what you did last week and *how awful it was…and you still can't believe what you said…how embarrassing…and no wonder he hasn't texted you since…because what on earth must he think of you now…you'll just have to avoid him forever…*

And on and on it goes.

Does this sound familiar?

So the big question is, are you in control of your thoughts, or do they control you?

The three F's and the primitive brain

Sometimes, however, it's helpful to have thoughts that take control… especially if you're facing an immediate threat. Our brains have developed so that we can respond without thinking when we need to.

A few years ago I was in a hotel fire in the middle of the night in Paris. The alarm sounded. I jumped out of bed, opened the door and looked into the smoke-filled corridor. At that point I didn't stop and think about anything. I didn't stop to think about what I should do next, if I should pack up my belongings or grab my passport. I didn't debate which staircase to take. I didn't think about my messy bed hair or putting on my shoes. I didn't think of taking my coat to keep me warm in the cold night air. In fact, I didn't think at all. I responded instinctively. Thinking would have taken up precious time and energy in the face of danger. I followed the emergency lights along the corridor and ran.

In that moment the primitive part of my brain took over. This is a part of the human brain that is wired to respond to serious threat and danger. It is this instinctive brain that responds quickly and without thinking that has helped us to survive.

So back in the day, when we lived in caves and faced real danger on a daily basis, we needed to act quickly by either fighting the threat, fleeing from it fast, or staying very still and hoping the danger would pass us by. This is called the *fight, flight or freeze* response, or the three F's. So that night in the hotel, my fight, flight or freeze response automatically kicked in and told me the best thing to do was run. Fast. The primitive part of my brain did the thinking for me, allowing me to focus all my energy and resources on reaching safety (and by the way, everyone's primitive brains in the hotel were working well that night because we all got out in one piece).

But situations like this are rare. We don't face fires every day.

The trouble is, our brains can act as if we do, and our primitive brain takes over even when it doesn't need to.

A bit more about brain science

There's still so much we don't yet know about how the brain works, but in the past 100 years or so, we've found out a lot more about how it has developed and how it functions.

Let's think of the human brain as being made up of two main parts, the lower brain and the upper brain. At birth the lower brain is quite well formed because its job is to do the automatic things that keep us alive, things like breathing, keeping the heart beating and controlling functions like sleep and digesting food. It is also this lower brain that helps us to survive when we detect danger, by responding quickly with the fight, flight or freeze response. It works much faster than any other part of the brain and isn't something we consciously think about. Most animals share this type of primitive brain with us…even birds and reptiles. This part of the brain also houses a small almond-shaped structure called the amygdala, which is responsible for emotional responses. So it's thanks to the amygdala that we feel a whole range of emotions such as happy, scared, angry, tearful or excited. When you flip out and scream at the person who behaved as if you didn't exist and pushed in front of you, that's your emotional amygdala taking over. Your primitive brain is responding as if you're under real threat, rather than that you've just missed your turn in the queue.

The upper brain isn't so well developed at birth, and it develops and refines as we grow and interact with other people. This upper brain is what makes us different from other animals and what makes us human. The upper brain is our conscious thinking brain, and neuroscientists think it is this bit that helps us think, work things out, remember, plan and pay attention to more than one thing at a time.

When we are born the upper and lower parts of the brain aren't well connected, and it is vital that babies get the experiences, opportunities and care that enable the connections between the two parts of the brain to develop and grow. These connections, or neuronal pathways, are a bit like a road system around a busy city. Some of these roads will be well used, wide and fast, like a four-lane motorway. They have clear directions and signs and link up with other equally fast road networks. They are well used and well maintained. But other roads won't be used very much at all; they're slow and difficult to navigate and will wear away like dirt tracks that fade in the mud.

Why do we need efficient connections, or fast and efficient roadways between the two brains?

Remember that the lower brain acts quickly and instinctively to keep us safe, triggering the fight, flight or freeze response. Sometimes the lower brain can kick in when we don't actually need it to and we rely on the thinking, rational upper brain to calm it down and help us to make decisions and think more clearly. After all, thankfully for most of us there won't be many occasions when our life is actually under threat in the modern world. The trouble is our brain can act as if we are. So when someone pushes in front of you in the queue, your lower brain can kick in, screaming at you to stay and fight or run and hide. In these situations we rely on our upper thinking brain to act like a pause button, and to help us make the decision about whether we are under real threat or not, whether we actually need to fight or flee, or if it's okay to stop and think a bit more about what we want to do.

Remember those unhelpful thoughts that can take over and make us feel and behave in a way we don't want to? Our unhelpful thoughts can act like roadblocks and stop messages getting from the upper to the lower brain.

Can you think of a time when your primitive brain took over when there was no real threat to your life? Here's what the Workout Team said. Try to work out which of the three F's kicked in, in each example:

> Everyone turned to stare when I walked into class late, which made me drop my bag. They were all laughing and sniggering, and I felt so stupid – I just wanted to get out of there. I went bright red and I felt sick.

Is this fight, flight or freeze?

> This morning when the bus driver rolled his eyes and tutted at me for not having the right change I wanted to scream. How dare he disrespect me like that! I wanted to tell him exactly where to go...that would have wiped that smug look from his face.

Is this fight, flight or freeze?

Neither of these situations is exactly pleasant, but nor are they life-threatening. Sometimes, just *thinking* about something can make your body react as if it's a serious threat by:

→ Preparing you to *fight*: stress hormones make your heart beat faster and your veins throb as blood is pumped around your body so you're ready to square up to the attack.

→ Preparing you for *flight*: stress hormones increase the blood flow to your limbs and release sugar in your blood so that you are ready to run.

→ Preparing you to *freeze*: stress hormones create a feeling of clamming up, light-headedness and going blank, so you can stay extra still to assess the danger.

And if this becomes a habit, then unhelpful thoughts might be taking over.

Unhelpful thoughts act like they're something they're not

Frenemy thoughts ooze confidence. They don't suffer from self-doubt, and they have ideas way, way above their station. In fact, most of the time unhelpful frenemy thoughts behave as if they're facts and not just thoughts.

But thoughts are not facts; they're just thoughts.

A fact is something that can be proven to be true. A fact is not an opinion, it is not a belief and it is certainly not a thought.

A thought is just a thought…although it can do a pretty good job of dressing itself up as a fact.

The Workout Team tried out some things whenever they noticed an unhelpful thought. Here are some of the things they tried:

I ask myself if it is true some of the time, all of the time or never…

I look at the evidence for and against the thought and try to weigh it up, as if I am in a court and have to prove the truth.

I check out what else has happened that might be making me feel this way – am I blowing it up because I've had a bad day?

I try to think of other options...it might be true but then again, it might not be...I try to think of as many alternatives as I can...

Sometimes I try to make fun of the thought...I say it in a silly voice or give it a daft or rude name. That way it doesn't seem to bother me so much.

When you notice unhelpful thoughts, remember to recognise them for what they are – frenemy thoughts!

Unhelpful thoughts hate the word 'yet'

Unhelpful frenemy thoughts love a 'can't-do' attitude. They're the opposite of your personal cheerleaders – they're the ones who stand on the sidelines to jeer you down. They make a big song and dance about what you can't do. Unhelpful thoughts might say things like:

I'm just no good at it…

I'm not that smart…clever…attractive…funny…

I can't cope with pressure…

I've never been able to…sing…do maths problems…juggle…

It's just the way I am…once I've opened a packet of biscuits I can't stop…

Now try adding the word 'yet' to those thoughts and notice what happens. It changes the emphasis entirely, doesn't it? Who knew such a little word could have such power? By adding the word 'yet', we're adding possibility. We're acknowledging that some things might not come easy to us, but with time and effort, who knows?

I've never been able to juggle…yet…

The word 'yet' acknowledges that nothing is fixed and set in stone. We can change. Yes, perhaps I've never been able to juggle, but if I practise every day for a month, who knows? It may take a while, and I'll probably make many mistakes along the way. At times I might even look quite silly. But in time, and with effort, I will be able to improve my juggling skills. In other words, adding the word 'yet' can push unhelpful and stuck thoughts from a fixed mindset into a growth mindset.

A fixed mindset believes in labels and looks for ways to confirm that those labels are right. So, with a fixed mindset, failing at something simply confirms that you're no good at it. However, a growth mindset believes that the talents we're born with are just a starting point, and that putting in effort and learning from mistakes are vital for success and achievement. A growth mindset sees failing as an opportunity to learn and improve.

You'll never catch frenemy thoughts using the word 'yet'. It's just not in their mindset!

Keeping your enemies closer...

Now that we know a few facts about unhelpful thinking habits, we can start to explore our own thoughts, and think about how we can get to know them better.

Ever heard the saying, 'Keep your best friends close but keep your enemies closer'? It sounds like nonsense, doesn't it? Keep an enemy closer than a best friend? What kind of advice is that? I don't think so!

But perhaps we should think again…

The closer you keep someone the more you get to know and understand them. And when you understand them, you know what they're capable of and you're more able to predict what they're likely to do. Ultimately, this will give you more choices about what *you* want to do.

It's the same with your thoughts. And it can be helpful to keep frenemy thoughts close, by getting to know them.

But isn't there a simpler solution to this? Why can't we just ditch the frenemy thought altogether? Why would we want to keep unhelpful thoughts close instead of simply getting rid of them? Wouldn't that make much more sense?

Unfortunately life's not always that simple…and wiping something totally out of your life is easier said than done. Often, the more you try to block or ignore something, the more it seems to pop up everywhere.

Ever had the words of a song or tune stuck in your mind, and the more you try to ignore it the stronger and louder it becomes, and the more agitated and irritated you feel?

Usually, it's only when you relax and stop trying to ignore it that it disappears! How ironic!

It can be exactly the same with your thoughts, and trying to ditch them may not be the answer. And occasionally even an unhelpful frenemy thought has its uses.

Ever had a friend who can be both a best friend and a frenemy at the same time? While you might not want to ditch this person altogether, you do need to be able to recognise and accept them for who and what they are…so you can take the good with bad, and accept that sometimes they will be the person you need to listen to, and sometimes the one you need to ignore. And even when they're saying something you don't want to hear, occasionally a frenemy can help you think about things differently.

Sometimes we need thoughts that take control and help us to act fast, or sometimes they might say something that can help us understand things differently. Therefore wiping them out of your life may not always be the most useful solution. Perhaps, as the saying goes, it's more helpful to keep unhelpful frenemy thoughts closer.

By keeping them close you can get to know unhelpful thoughts better, so you can notice when they're trying to creep up and take you by surprise, allowing you to take back the controls and choose whether to listen to them…or not. And that's exactly what this book is all about.

Before we move on to look more closely at the link between our thoughts, feelings and behaviour, why not try some of the **Warming Up exercises** below to start getting to know your own thoughts, both the helpful and unhelpful ones, a little more?

WARMING UP

Sometimes you might want to let your mind wander and become lost in your thoughts, but at other times you might want to stop your thoughts taking you away from the here and now and dragging you to a place where you don't really want to be. You need to be able to notice your thoughts in the first place before you can decide what you want to do with them. These Warming Up exercises can help you become better at noticing your thoughts before you become carried away by them.

Just like it's good practice to warm up your muscles and notice how your body is feeling before a physical workout, getting into the habit of warming up your thoughts can help you become more aware of them, and know what is normal for you.

Remember to do some Warming Up exercises every day to help you check in with your thinking habits. Try to notice:

- *When do you mind-wander?* Start noticing your thoughts when you're doing everyday things like brushing your teeth, having a drink, taking a bus or a car ride, going for a walk, making breakfast or preparing a sandwich for your lunch, for example. Try to notice what you are doing when you become lost in your thoughts.

- *Where do your mind-wandering thoughts take you?* The present, the past or the future? Are you thinking about things that are happening in that precise moment? The taste of the toothpaste as it hits your tongue? The different sounds you can hear as you sit on the bus? The feel of the wind and the smell of the traffic as you walk to school?

  Or maybe your mind wanders somewhere far more pleasant? Perhaps it takes you to your favourite holiday destination…a warm sunny beach, or a place where you feel safe and happy?

  Or perhaps your thoughts take you back to the past or into the future? Do they re-play something you've already said or done, or do they try to predict what is going to happen? Are these helpful or unhelpful thoughts?

  Do you choose what you want to think about or where your thoughts wander? Or do you find yourself thinking these things before you've realised?

- *What do your thoughts say?* Try to write some of your actual thoughts down. Do they sound like a best friend…or a frenemy?

- *How do your thoughts make you feel?* Try to notice if your thoughts cause any strong feelings. For example, do they make you feel happy, relaxed, calm, or worried, angry, distressed, nervous, ashamed? Anything else?

- *Where do you notice these feelings in your body?* Perhaps you notice big feelings like anger or worry in your stomach or your head or throat? Or maybe you feel hot or cold, or tense or shaky. Try to notice where you feel emotions, and how these responses in your body might be linked to your thoughts.

    Don't worry if you're not sure what you are thinking about when you are mind-wandering. That is totally normal. Just try to notice over the next few days and make a note of what happens.

- *Try to notice the here and now.* Try to notice what is happening around you, this very minute! Remember that unhelpful thoughts don't like the here and now, and tend to drag us into the past or propel us into the future. Practise noticing the here and now so you will be able to take some control. Spend five minutes concentrating on the here and now and the things around you. Try to notice:

    - Your breathing.

    - The sounds around you.

    - The smells around you.

    - The different range of tastes when you're eating or drinking.

    - The feel and sensations of your body as you're sitting, lying or moving around.

Don't worry if you find it hard to focus on the here and now, and if you drift into thoughts and daydreams. Remember that it is really hard to break old habits and make new ones, so you'll probably fall into old ways of thinking without realising. That's fine. Just try to notice the thought as it happens, then gently re-focus on the here and now. It's also okay if you find it a bit weird or a bit boring or uncomfortable. In fact, that's entirely normal.

- Practise being in the here and now by naming:

  - 5 things you can see.

  - 4 things you can hear.

  - 3 things you can touch.

  - 2 things you can smell.

  - 1 thing you can taste.

Try to do this exercise at different times during your day.

- Try noticing the here and now when you want to bring your focus back. If you're feeling overwhelmed by a big or difficult feeling, such as worry or anxiety, anger or sadness, try to re-focus on what is happening around you and what is happening in your body. For example, is your breathing becoming faster, or are your muscles becoming tight and tense? Try to become aware of the link between what you think, what you feel and where you feel it. Being able to stay in the here and now can help you to notice when big thoughts and feelings are taking over, making it more likely that you can decide what you'd like to do next.

UNHELPFUL THOUGHTS IN ACTION

MARC'S MISERABLE MORNING

Marc got out of the wrong side of the bed this morning, didn't he?

It all started with the empty juice carton in the fridge, and then his thoughts and feelings spiralled out of control until he became so frustrated that he ended up picking a fight with the fridge. But it didn't stop there... his morning seemed to go from bad to worse...

Unsurprisingly he didn't win the fight with the fridge and he really hurt his foot. It was still throbbing when he left for school and he had to hobble slowly to the bus stop. He got there just as the bus was pulling away. Because his foot was aching so badly he couldn't walk to school and he had to wait for the next bus. As luck would have it, the next bus was late so Marc was really, really late for his first lesson. Mr Chilvers gave him a lunchtime detention and wouldn't listen to any of his excuses! Because of his detention, Marc was last in the lunchtime queue, and by the time he got served there were no toasties or pizzas left. He had to have a dry cheese sandwich. Not his favourite! Thankfully, after lunch his foot was feeling a bit better and he was able to play football with his mates. Afterwards Marc found that his frustration and anger had worn off a bit and he began to feel a bit stupid for getting so het up about the juice carton that morning. It's only juice after all! He began to think about how his reaction to it had maybe made everything even worse...

The power of unhelpful thoughts

Let's think about Marc's morning a little more. And especially the part his thoughts played in it. Can you spot how Marc's thoughts:

→ Took control...before he realised?

→ Dragged him back to the past?

→ Acted like they were facts?

→ Took on a 'can't do' attitude?

Make a note of your ideas here.

```
┌────────────────────────────────────────────────────┐
│                                                    │
│                                                    │
│                                                    │
│                                                    │
└────────────────────────────────────────────────────┘

┌────────────────────────────────────────────────────┐
│                                                    │
│                                                    │
│                                                    │
│                                                    │
└────────────────────────────────────────────────────┘

┌────────────────────────────────────────────────────┐
│                                                    │
│                                                    │
│                                                    │
│                                                    │
└────────────────────────────────────────────────────┘
```

Let's see what the Workout Team said:

His thoughts took over as soon as he saw the empty carton – all he could think about was blaming his brother.

His frenemy thoughts left no room for any other reasons about why the empty carton was there. They acted like facts, saying his brother had left it there to annoy him. But what if he didn't? What if his brother was in a rush and just didn't think about what he was doing…or what if he'd been disturbed by his mother calling him or his phone ringing? And what if it wasn't his brother at all? What if his mum had left the carton there?

Marc's thoughts got stuck on all of the other times his brother has done things to annoy him.

His thoughts made him compare himself in a negative way. They got stuck on how other people don't treat him fairly, and how his brother has it so much easier than him…

Marc's unhelpful thoughts made him feel helpless and he got stuck on loop about life being unfair…

As we have seen, Marc's unhelpful thinking habits acted very fast, took over his thinking and he quickly became very angry. His thoughts about the empty carton focused on how unfair the situation was, and led to all the other times life had been unfair to him. So Marc grew angrier and angrier. His thoughts made his body feel as if he was under attack. So his body got ready to respond to the attack. In this case, Marc became ready to fight. The problem was, there was no one to fight! So Marc fought the fridge…and came off worse! Marc's unhelpful frenemy thoughts directly affected his feelings, which then affected his behaviour.

None of this made the situation any better. It certainly didn't mean Marc got his glass of juice. All Marc ended up with was a very sore foot and a morning that was hijacked by his angry and frustrated feelings. And his unhelpful thoughts kept those negative feelings going all morning – because that's what they're good at.

But what if Marc had noticed his unhelpful thoughts before they took over? What if he'd kept his frenemy thoughts close? What if we could re-write Marc's morning? What if he'd thought about things in a different way? What might those thoughts have been? Jot them in your workout notes or on your phone.

And if Marc had thought in a different way, how might this have changed his behaviour and his morning? Write your ideas down.

[Blank box]

[Blank box]

[Blank box]

If Marc had noticed his unhelpful thoughts, he could have:

→ Gone along with them. He could have noticed the thought, 'My brother's such a pain and he only does this to wind me up,' and instead of letting the thought take control, Marc could have accepted the thought just as it is:

> Yes, my brother's a pain and there's not much I can do about that. And yes, maybe he's doing this to wind me up. But I can't change my brother or the things that he does. However, it doesn't have to affect me. I can notice my thoughts about him and let them go. I can accept that sometimes that's just the way it is.

→ Challenged them. He could have noticed the thought, 'My brother's such a pain and he only does this to wind me up,' and he could have questioned it:

> Yes, maybe it's true that he's done this on purpose to make me mad, but then again, maybe it's not. I don't know for sure. Perhaps there are other reasons why he left the empty carton in the fridge.

Maybe he was thinking about his football match tonight or maybe mum called him and he simply forgot. And even if he did it on purpose this time, is it really true that he only does things to wind me up ALL of the time?

Left unnoticed, unhelpful thinking habits can run wild. And when they run wild and out of control they can trigger a fight, flight or freeze response. If this happens regularly it can make you feel as if you are constantly being hijacked by big and difficult feelings like anger, sadness, worry, fear or anxiety. Over time this can really affect your behaviour…and your life. In other words, left unnoticed, unhelpful frenemy thoughts can affect your mental health.

Marc realised his unhelpful thinking habits were taking over and affecting him negatively. He wanted to get his thinking habits in shape. Here's how he put this into action using the Mental Health and Wellbeing Workout.

How Marc created his Mental Health and Wellbeing Workout

→ Marc looked back at the **Warming Up exercises** in Chapter 1. He made a note of them on his phone and decided he would use them to help him get better at noticing his thoughts, both helpful and unhelpful. He set his alarm to remind him to do his **exercises** each day.

→ Marc read though the **Stretch and Flex-ercise** section in Chapter 3 and tried out some of the ideas. He added his favourites to his own workout.

→ Over the next few weeks, Marc read through the chapters in Part 2 and got to know some of the common unhelpful thinking habits. He identified with quite a few of them. He wasn't worried, though, because he knew that unhelpful thoughts stick together!

→ Marc tried out some of the **Think-ercises** and added a few to his own workout.

➜ Marc then had his very own personalised Mental Health and Wellbeing Workout. He tried to make a new habit by doing his workout every day. He found it helpful to do it at the same time and place. Soon, he found that he was becoming much more aware of his thinking habits and that sometimes just noticing them and accepting them was enough to make them matter less.

➜ Marc also remembered to fill his mental health gym bag with all the other things that help his wellbeing too, with the ideas from the Introduction.

STRETCH AND FLEX-ERCISES

Change the way you think about things so the things that you think about change.

Stretch and Flex-ercises can help you to notice and accept your unhelpful thoughts and will give you ideas for responding to them more flexibly. Remember – the aim isn't to get rid of the thoughts, but to help you have more awareness and choice in how you respond.

What is flexible thinking and how does it affect mental wellbeing?

Being more flexible with your thoughts means you have more choice about what you do next, so you will be less likely to be hijacked by big and difficult feelings. Remember how Marc's thoughts about the empty juice carton took him back to the past, hijacked his thinking and created big angry feelings? His unhelpful thoughts were rigid and inflexible. They didn't allow him to think of any alternatives. They quickly flipped him into fight mode, and stopped him from thinking of his other options, narrowing his choices.

Inflexible or rigid thinking like Marc's can cause big and uncomfortable feelings, which can then affect what you say and what you do. If this happens over and over again, it can be bad news for your mental health, perhaps causing you to feel more irritable, sad, angry, low, anxious…

However, flexible thinking isn't about dismissing or getting rid of the unhelpful thought; it's about noticing and accepting the unhelpful thought while also making room for other options. If Marc had been thinking more flexibly, he would have noticed his angry thoughts about his brother, but before they took up all of the space in his mind he would have considered some of the other possibilities too.

Practice makes perfect…

Thinking flexibly can take some practice. Remember a few things about unhelpful frenemy thoughts in Chapter 1? Unhelpful thoughts are fast, take over quickly and act like facts. This can make flexible thinking and noticing the unhelpful thought quite tricky. But recognising the unhelpful thought before it takes over is important – even if it does take a little practice.

Take a look at the **Stretch and Flex-ercises** on the next page. Start off by committing to one or two and add these to your **Warming Up exercises**. Try to do them every day at least once for a few minutes… or more if you can!

When we're trying to do something different or establish a new habit it can be helpful to practise the new thing at the same time every day, so try this with your **Stretch and Flex-ercises**. It might help if you find somewhere comfortable and distraction-free, so try to turn off your computer, television and phone while you're Flex-ercising!

Stretch and Flex-ercises

- **Practise flexible thinking**

  Over the next week try to:

  ☑ See the other side of an argument or opinion.

  ☑ Stand in someone else's shoes and see things from their point of view.

  ☑ Ask someone how something is making them feel.

  ☑ Think of as many different solutions to a problem as you can, no matter how wacky they sound.

  ☑ Purposely *don't* try to win an argument.

  ☑ Try to compromise and find the middle ground over something.

  See how many times you can do these things. Note how it makes you feel!

- **Notice unhelpful thoughts...and let them come and go**

Try not to become focused on ditching the thought, because that might make it stick faster. Why not try to notice your thoughts as they happen, accepting that they will come and go, and that you don't have to do anything with them. Try noticing and naming the thoughts: '...ah there's that thought about the science lesson again...it's just a thought, nothing else...'

Make a note in your workout notes or on your phone each time you notice unhelpful thoughts. You could do this at the end of the day or at different times during your day. Try to establish the habit of noticing and writing the unhelpful thoughts down. Perhaps try out some of the following phrases:

There it is again. It's a normal thought to have in this situation.

I don't have to agree or disagree with it.

I don't have to respond. I can do nothing.

I can write it down and leave it for later.

I don't have to stop this thought. It's okay for it to have its say.

It's just a thought.

I can sit this one out.

It will pass.

- **Notice the unhelpful thoughts...and accept (or agree with) them**

Accept that everyone has unhelpful thoughts from time to time. Sometimes they take hold at certain times, perhaps when you're tired or hungry or feeling unwell. Or maybe there are certain situations that trigger these thoughts for you. Try to identify and become more aware of the situations when you are most likely to have unhelpful thoughts.

Accept that these thoughts are just thoughts. They don't make you who you are or define you. You have these thoughts because you are human. Nothing else. Just because you have these thoughts, it doesn't mean that you have to act on them or do what they say. Try telling yourself you will observe and watch the thought without taking part in it. Try to wait for it to pass.

For example, you might tell yourself, 'Okay, there's that negative thought again telling me I'm stupid and making a fool of myself. I'll watch out for it in the future. It often happens when I'm speaking out in front of other people. I wonder if I'll spot it in any other situations too? Doesn't mean it's true, though. It's just a thought that is running through my mind. Everyone has thoughts like this sometimes, including me. It's part of being human.'

Perhaps you can try agreeing with the thought: 'I hear you and perhaps you're right…you've got a point…you're right, sometimes.'

How does that feel? Remember, even if the thought is partly right, you still don't have to act on it or do anything. Let the unhelpful thought have its say and see if this makes a difference.

- **Notice the unhelpful thoughts...and rate them**

When you notice the unhelpful thought, try to rate it on a scale of 1–10, by asking yourself:

☑ How strong is it today?

☑ How important is this to me right now?

☑ How important will it be to me in an hour? A day? A week? A month? A year?

- **Notice the unhelpful thoughts...and play around with them**

Make the unhelpful thought less important by having some fun with it. Try playing around with the thought. Ask yourself:

☑ If the thought were a colour, what colour would it be today?

☑ If the thought had an accent, what accent would it be using today?

☑ How is the thought moving? Is it fast, slow, wobbling…?

☑ If the thought had a smell, what would it be?

Part 2

Part 2

SOCIAL COMPARISON
(AKA THE SELF-HATER)

What is social comparison?

Comparing yourself to others is a natural and normal thing to do. We probably do it several times a day – often without realising.

Way back in the 1950s, a psychologist called Leon Festinger studied social comparison. He said:

There exists in the human organism a drive to evaluate his opinions and abilities.[1]

Meaning:

All humans compare themselves to each other. It helps us to understand who we are and what we're good at.

So comparing ourselves with others can be a helpful thing to do. It can help us to see our own positives more clearly, help us feel good about our skills and abilities or the effort we have put into something.

At other times we might compare ourselves to others in a negative way. We might think we aren't as good, talented or skilled as someone else. But even when we compare ourselves and come off worse, it doesn't

---

1   Festinger, L. (1954) 'A Theory of Social Comparison Processes.' *Human Relations 7* (2), 117–140.

have to be a bad thing. It can give us the push to want to do even better, try harder, practise more and focus on the things we want to improve. In this way, social comparison can be a good friend, giving us motivation and spurring us on to try new things, in new ways, to be the very best that we can be.

BUT…when social comparison gets out of control and we fall into the habit of comparing ourselves in an unhelpful, negative way, it can become a problem. Social comparison can be unhelpful when it sneaks up and points out all the things that we don't do particularly well, where we fall short, making us feel bad about ourselves. When this happens, social comparison can take over and become a familiar way of thinking.

Take Kye…

Kye has fallen into the habit of comparing himself to photos of Max on social media every day…and not in a good way. When he compares himself he always ends up feeling hopeless and not good enough in comparison to others. His habit of comparing himself doesn't energise him or make him want to do things differently – quite the opposite. It sucks out all of his energy and makes him feel really bad about himself. In other words, unhelpful social comparison is turning him into a self-hater!

And it has become such a habit for Kye that he usually doesn't even notice he's doing it, or notice the negative thoughts, until they've taken hold and he ends up feeling hopeless, inferior, angry, jealous, irritated and just plain fed up.

Social comparison has taken over.

You know it's an unhelpful thinking habit when…

Here are some thoughts from the Workout Team about social comparison. You know it's an unhelpful thinking habit when…

…you compare yourself negatively all the time and you can't see any positives about yourself.

…you always look at what's different or missing rather than what you've got in common with others.

…you make random and unrealistic comparisons, like comparing yourself to celebrities, famous people, and people who you don't know and will never meet. When you do this, you don't really know what you're comparing yourself to, and you're trying to live up to an image. It might not be the real thing.

…you keep making unfair comparisons. What if you think you're an okay singer until you compare yourself to a newly discovered singing sensation on YouTube? It might make you feel like you're not as good, and even feel as if you shouldn't be singing any more. But you're comparing yourself unfairly. All you can see and hear is what is in front of you. You don't know any of the facts…what it took for them to become that singer…how much practice, how many lessons, what

they might sound like on other days in other places…like the shower!
You don't know what they've done to get there or even if they've
changed their voice to make it seem better than it really is. It's not a true
comparison, is it?

Left unchecked, social comparison can negatively affect your mental health and wellbeing. Constantly thinking negative thoughts about yourself in comparison to others can make you feel not good enough, hopeless, angry and helpless. Eventually these feelings can affect what you do.

Remember the three F's (fight, flight or freeze) response in Chapter 1? Unhelpful social comparison can trigger your brain into believing you're under threat and that you need to fight the threat, or run away and hide. Constantly judging yourself in a negative way to others could leave you feeling helpless, hopeless and low. Constantly feeling this way, day in day out, can affect what you do. For example, feeling not good enough and helpless might make you less willing to take a risk and try new things.

If Kye continues to think things like, 'I'm no good, I'm not good enough, Max is so much better then me, I'll never be like that, so what's the point in trying?' this could make him feel:

Low, helpless, hopeless, angry, irritated.

And feeling this way could affect what he does. For example, he might:

Hide away, avoid going out and seeing his friends, give up trying to be the best he can be, pick fights with others, be short tempered and irritable…

Over time this will affect Kye's wellbeing, leaving him less able to switch off from the tough stuff and enjoy life. Social comparison could sap all of his mental strength.

Fitness test: Could social comparison be sapping your mental strength?

Read through the following statements and try to be as honest as you can. Perhaps talk them through with someone you trust.

1. Do you often find yourself thinking or saying things like:

   He's so much better than me at…

   She's so much more popular than me…

   Look at him; he's got it all…

   It's not fair… I'll never be that good at…

2. Do you find yourself:

   → Setting lower targets or goals than you should, just in case you can't do it?

   → Saying sorry all the time, as if everything is always your fault?

   → Being harder on yourself than you would your best friend?

   → Focusing on the 'can'ts' rather than the 'cans'?

   → Envying others? Regularly feeling envious, angry, inferior or jealous of someone?

   → Never measuring up as much as you want to?

   → Suffering from FOMO (fear of missing out)? (e.g. everyone seems to be having more fun than you, doing more exciting/meaningful/important/successful things, having a better life, etc.)?

We all might answer 'yes' to some of these statements from time to time, but be honest, how many would ring true for you on a regular basis?

If you're not sure about it, that's okay. It's not always easy to notice your thoughts. It takes some training and practice! Try to watch out for this unhelpful thinking habit over the next week.

Try to catch it in action, or spend some time at the end of each day thinking back. What happened? What did you notice? How did you feel? How did you respond to things? Was social comparison around?

Keep a note of any self-hating thoughts by writing them down in your workout notes or on your phone.

If you think social comparison is getting out of control and sapping your mental strength, choose some **Warming Up exercises**, **Stretch and**

Flex-ercises and **Think-ercises** to create your own Mental Health and Wellbeing Workout. The exercises you choose will depend on whether you want to focus on becoming more flexible and learning to live with the thought, or changing the shape of the thought itself.

Think-ercises

These Think-ercises can help you to challenge and change the thought over time, but it takes practice, and always begins with noticing when the thought is there.

1. Challenge and change your social comparisons

Start by making a note of your social comparisons. Try to notice:

- *Who are your usual social comparisons?* Make a list of the people you regularly compare yourself to. Think carefully about this as some of the comparisons might not be immediately obvious… they might be well hidden!

- *Do you compare yourself to people you actually see in person…real people you see and talk to…or do you mostly compare yourself to people you never meet?* Are your main comparisons the people who present a version of themselves online…like on Instagram and Snapchat?

- *Are your social comparisons realistic and helpful? Do they spur you on to try new things and make you hopeful? Or do they tend to make you feel inferior and hopeless?* Try to become more aware when you are falling into unhelpful social comparison habits.

Now try to limit the number of people you compare yourself to, and catch yourself comparing yourself to people you don't meet in person, or comparing yourself to an image presented on social media. When you catch yourself doing this, remember to *be kind to yourself*. We all compare ourselves to others all of the time! Try writing the thought down so you can get to know it better, and become more aware when it is creeping up on you.

Be your own social comparison and try to compare yourself with YOU! Think about:

- How you are doing today in comparison with how you were doing a day ago, a week ago, a month or even a year ago.

- Ask yourself how you want to be in the future and what steps you are going to take to make this happen.

2. Be your own best friend

Try to be your own best friend. When you notice the social comparison thought, ask yourself what a best friend would tell you, or what advice you would give to your best friend. Challenge unhelpful thinking by engaging your best friend. Ask yourself:

- Is this true? Is the person I am comparing myself to always like this? What evidence do I have? What evidence do I have that this is *not* always how they are?

- Is it true that I am always like this? What evidence do I have? When am I the same and when am I different?

- What are my good points? What would my best friend say about my strengths?

- Is there anything I can do right now to change this situation? Who and what can help me?

3. Divert the thought

Send the thought in a different direction by trying some of the following ideas:

- Write the unhelpful thought down when you spot it.

- Try to change the thought into a more helpful one. Write this down.

- Test the unhelpful thought. How true is it? Is it true all of the time, some of the time, never? What are the facts to support this? Will this matter as much in an hour, tomorrow, next week, next year?

- When you notice the unhelpful thought, try to do something different to divert it. This could be:

  ☑ Noticing and accepting the thought for what it is (it's just a thought).

  ☑ Bringing your focus back to the here and now (what five things can you hear/see/smell around you right now?).

  ☑ Doing something physical like going for a walk, listening or dancing to music, getting a cold glass of water and drinking it very slowly, or concentrating on your breathing for a few minutes.

Find what works best for you in diverting the thought.

Kye's Mental Health and Wellbeing Workout

Take Kye, after his workout.

Kye decided the social comparison frenemy was getting out of control. He chose a combination of **Stretch and Flex-ercises** and **Think-ercises**.
Here's what his workout looked like.

WARMING UP

- *Practise being in the here and now*. I will practise paying attention to my breathing and the sounds around me. I'll try to do this for five minutes when I am in the car travelling to and from school, and before I go to sleep at night.

Stretch and Flex-ercises

- *Practise noticing* each time I slip into social comparison. When I look at Facebook or Instagram I will watch out for unhelpful social comparison thoughts. I will keep a note in my workout pages or on my phone every time a social comparison slips into self-hating. When I notice it I will say hello to the thought, and remind myself that I don't have to do anything. It's just a thought, nothing else.

- *Accept the thought*. When I notice the social comparison thought I'll try to accept that it is going to appear now and again. I'll say to myself, 'There it is again. It's okay. This kind of thinking often appears when I'm looking at selfies. That's totally normal for me.'

Think-ercises

- I will *notice and keep a list* of my social comparisons. I like making diagrams and charts, so I'll make a chart of the social comparisons that are part of my actual, everyday life, and those that are on social media or on TV.

- I will try to become *my own social comparison*. At the end of each week I will write down one thing I'm pleased with, one thing I've tried to do differently, and one thing I want to do even better.

- *Test the unhelpful thoughts.* I will write down the unhelpful thought and then test it:

  Max looks great. He always looks better than me.

  Is that true? Does he really look great? Or does he look good, quite good or okay? Does he look great all of the time? How do I know this? What are the facts? Does he always look better than me? Is this a fact? Does he sometimes look better than me, and sometimes not?

  How important is it to me right now that Max looks better than me? On a scale of 1–10, how much does this matter? How much will it matter in an hour? Tomorrow? Next week? Next year?

CATASTROPHISING

(AKA BUT WHAT IF...)

What is catastrophising?

Sometimes bad things happen. It's part of life to face difficult situations and events. So occasionally it can be helpful to prepare yourself for the tough stuff, especially if it helps you rehearse how to get through it, should the worst actually come true. Anticipating and problem-solving can be a helpful thing to do.

BUT…sometimes our thoughts can become fixated on the bad stuff, and how awful and difficult things can be. We can become so fixated that the fear of something bad happening takes hold and blows up out of proportion. And then it's the *fear* of something bad happening that becomes the thing that keeps the difficult feelings alive.

This kind of thinking can become a problem because it creates strong, unpleasant feelings about things that might never actually happen in real life.

Although bad things can happen, it doesn't mean that they will!

This thinking is sometimes called 'catastrophising'. Catastrophising is usually made up of two parts:

→ Overestimating the likelihood that something bad is going to happen.

→ Underestimating your ability to cope if the bad thing actually comes true.

Take Tia…

When Tia is asked to stay behind after class, she immediately begins to catastrophise and imagines all of the negative reasons why: she's made a mess of her homework, she's not clever enough, she'll be put down a set…

Then she jumps to the conclusion that if this actually happens it will be an absolute catastrophe and she won't be able to cope, she won't know anyone in that class and she will be an outcast.

Mark Twain, a famous American author born way back in 1835, recognised this unhelpful thinking habit a long time ago when he said:

> *I am an old man and I have known a great many troubles…but most of them never happened.*

Like Mark Twain, if Tia isn't careful she will fall into the unhelpful habit of stressing over things that might never happen.

You know it's an unhelpful thinking habit when…

Here are some thoughts from the Workout Team about catastrophising. You know it's an unhelpful thinking habit when…

> *…you find yourself imagining the very worst that could happen in every situation.*

> *…the negative things take up all the space in your mind.*

> *…you focus on how difficult things are going to be.*

> *…your thoughts often start with…'but what if…' and 'it's probably…' and end with the worst case scenario.*

> *…you feel as if you're living in a state of constant anxiety, worry and fear about the things that might happen.*

> *…you constantly doubt your ability to cope.*

> *…you tend to forget about all of the other times when you've got through tough stuff, or think they don't count.*

Left unnoticed catastrophising can play havoc with your mental health and wellbeing. Constantly over-focusing on the likelihood of negative things happening and believing you won't be able to cope can leave you feeling helpless, afraid, anxious and exhausted. In turn these feelings can affect what you do. For example, worrying about the likelihood of bad stuff happening can leave you feeling too afraid to try anything at all and in danger of missing out on many brilliant experiences…and even life itself!

Remember the fight, flight or freeze response in Chapter 1? Unhelpful catastrophising thoughts can leave the lower brain in a persistent state of alertness, permanently wired for disaster, and unable to engage effectively with our thinking upper brain. Because catastrophising predicts the worst, the lower brain responds by getting us ready to address the disaster either by getting ready to fight, running away or becoming immobilised or frozen. As it does so, we are flooded with stress hormones to keep us alert and on guard. Persistent unhelpful thinking like catastrophising can leave us with big feelings of anxiety, worry, agitation or anger in a body that's ready for a danger that might never happen!

If Tia continues to worry about things that might never happen, how bad and awful they might be, and fretting about how she'll be able to cope, this could make her feel:

Anxious, scared, sad, helpless, hopeless, angry, irritated…

And feeling this way could affect what she does. For example, she might feel increasingly worried about her ability to cope and get through things, and therefore avoid situations *just in case* she finds them difficult. This means she will have less experience of different situations, where she can discover she actually *can* cope! Her confidence and self-belief will wither away, and she will shut herself off from people and situations even more. She will try to cope with her difficult feelings in unhealthy and unhelpful ways. Over time this will affect Tia's wellbeing, leaving her less able to switch off from the bad stuff and enjoy life. Catastrophising could sap all of her mental strength.

Fitness test: Could catastrophising be sapping your mental strength?

Read through the following statements and try to be as honest as you can. Perhaps talk them through with someone you trust.

1. Do you often find yourself predicting the very worst that could happen, and then convincing yourself it will be a total disaster? Things like:

   I can't believe I said that/did that…they are going to be so mad with me…they'll probably never speak to me ever again…then no one will want to have anything to do with me…

   I've made so many mistakes there's no way I'm going to pass it now and I'll never get into college, then I'll be stuck in a dead end job with no qualifications…

2. Do you find yourself underestimating your ability to cope with the tough stuff? Thinking things like:

   …and I'll never be able to make any new friends ever again.

   …and I'll have to do a job I hate for the rest of my life.

3. When you notice your thoughts, do you find yourself thinking words or phrases like:

   But what if…

   It's probably…

   I always…

   It's the worst thing ever…

   I can't cope…

   I'll never be able to…

   It's a disaster…

4. You believe if you imagine the very worst that could happen that it is a kind of protection. If you think of the worst then it won't actually happen…

We all might answer 'yes' to some of these statements from time to time, but be honest, how many of these statements would ring true for you on a regular basis?

If you're not sure about it, that's okay. As I mentioned before, it's not always easy to notice your thoughts. It takes some training! Try to watch out for catastrophising thoughts over the next week or so. Try to catch the thoughts in action, or spend some time at the end of each day thinking back. What happened? What did you notice? How did you feel? How did you respond to things? Keep a note of any catastrophising thoughts that blow things out of proportion by writing them down in your workout notes or on your phone.

If you think catastrophising is getting out of control and sapping your mental strength, have a look at the **Think-ercises** below. Perhaps add some of these to your **Warming Up exercises** and **Stretch and Flex-ercises** to make your own personal workout.

Think-ercises

You might decide that you want to challenge the thought. These Think-ercises will help to change the shape of the thought over time, but it takes practice, and always starts by noticing by the unhelpful thought first!

1. Look for perspective

- Challenge yourself to distinguish between catastrophes/disasters and things that are difficult and unpleasant. For example, failing an exam may be difficult and unpleasant, but is it a true disaster? Failing an exam doesn't mean that you are doomed to fail everything for the rest of your life.

☑ Write down your catastrophising thought. Now try to rate how true the thought is using the 'Ladder of Truth':

☑ Draw a ladder with ten rungs. The bottom rung is true all of the time, the top rung is never true. Where would you put the unhelpful thought?

☑ Where might other people place the thought if you asked them; for example, your good friends, your family, your teachers…?

☑ Re-write the thought so that it reflects more truth.

- Trigger words can act like a fuse for the catastrophising thought. Stop the thought from blowing up by refusing to light the fuse:

☑ Look out for trigger words that blow things up such as always, never, won't and can't.

☑ Do these trigger words exaggerate the thought and make things seem even worse?

☑ What words can you use to give it more perspective? Make a list. They might include sometimes, occasionally, might, possibly.

☑ Re-write the thought using some of the perspective-giving words.

2. Challenge the thought

- Is the thought a fact or an opinion? Remember that facts are true and have proof, whereas opinions may be true or false and don't have any proof. What proof do you have that this thought is a fact? Or is it just a thought?

3. Play around with the thought

- Write down the catastrophising thought and play around with it by thinking of all the different possible outcomes:

☑ Imagine all of the possible outcomes that could happen, the negative ones as well as any positives. Instead of thinking of just one outcome, see how many different outcomes you can come up with.

☑ Now look at all the different outcomes and see which ones are true catastrophes, which ones are very unpleasant, which ones are unpleasant, which ones aren't too bad at all and which ones are positive.

☑ Play around with the original thought to reflect some of the other possible outcomes too.

4. Become a problem solver

• Think about the things you could do if the worst actually did happen:

☑ For example, if you failed your exam, what could you do? Could you talk to a teacher about your options? Could you take a re-sit? Could you do extra studying?

☑ Is it true that you *never* cope? Can you think of a time when you've coped even though it may have been difficult? Think about any other times when difficult things have happened and what you did to get through it. Can you draw on any past experiences?

5. Connect with your best friend

• Talk to the friends you trust and ask what they think, or be your own best friend and consider what you would tell someone if they were having these thoughts.

Tia's Mental Health and Wellbeing Workout

Take Tia, after her workout.

Tia decided that catastrophising was getting out of control. She chose a combination of **Stretch and Flex-ercises** and **Think-ercises** to add to her **Warming Up exercises**.

This is what she put in her workout.

WARMING UP

- I will try to choose when I want to listen to my thoughts and when I want to stay in the here and now. I will especially try to stay in the here and now when I am feeling stressed and worried about something that might happen. I will *practise staying in the here and now* by trying to notice the sounds, smells and sensations around me. I will also try to notice where I feel stress and worry in my body.

Stretch and Flex-ercises

- When I notice the catastrophising thought I won't worry about it and I will try to *let it come and go*. I will remember that it is just a thought and it won't last forever. I'll try not to become too worried about stopping the thought as this might just make it even stronger, so instead I will try to tell myself:

  There's the catastrophising thought again. That's okay. It's a normal thought to have in this situation.

  I don't have to agree or disagree with it.

  I don't have to respond. I can do nothing.

  I can write it down and leave it for later.

  I don't have to stop this thought. It's okay for it to have its say.

  I will write these phrases in my workout notes or on my phone so I get can into the habit of using them.

Think-ercises

- *I will try to look for some perspective.* I will write down the catastrophising thought when I notice it and I'll place the thought on the Ladder of Truth, remembering to think of how realistic the thought actually is and where other people would place it on the ladder. I'll try to remember to be realistic about the things that are true disasters and things that are just unpleasant and difficult.

- I am going to try to become more of a *problem-solver* and think about how I could cope if bad things happen. There are times in the past when I've got through some really hard times, like when my parents split up, when I've fallen out with friends and when I've failed tests or coursework, and although it was tough I got through them all. I'll try to think about all the different things I can do to manage and cope.

BLACK-AND-WHITE THINKING
(AKA ALL-OR-NOTHING THINKING)

What is black-and-white thinking?

Black-and-white thinking is sometimes called all-or-nothing thinking or rigid thinking because it doesn't allow any room for other possibilities. When we engage in black-and-white thinking we tend to see things in extremes and forget that there are a range of possibilities in between.

Occasionally, it can be helpful to think in simple black-and-white terms. When we are faced with a threat, we need to be able to make quick decisions and respond fast. In the past this would have made it easier for our ancestors to make quick social decisions about who to trust and who to keep at a distance.

Black-and-white thinking can be particularly useful when we need to make decisions about our safety.

For example, Tiger on the loose – Bad – Run – Fast!

We all think in black-and-white terms from time to time, especially when we are young. It can be much simpler to view the world in an all-or-nothing, black-and-white way, and it can feel safer too. Very young children often find it easier to view the world in extremes as it can seem easier and less complicated; for example, friend or enemy, right or wrong, pass or fail. However, as we grow older we begin to understand that the world isn't quite so simple and things don't always fall clearly into discrete categories. Things or people are rarely all good or all bad all of the time. So although you might fail an exam, it doesn't mean *you* are a failure or that you've failed every single question in the exam! You may have passed certain questions or elements of the coursework. The truth is that most things in life aren't totally fantastic or total disasters. Most things in life have good bits, bad bits and all the so-so bits in between…

Black-and-white thinking can be unhelpful when it leads us to make simplistic and rash decisions too quickly, without considering the facts. Such all-or-nothing thinking can be narrow, restricted and doesn't help us see things as they really are.

If we get into the habit of thinking in black-and-white terms then this can become a problem. Unhelpful black-and-white thoughts are great at presenting themselves as facts and stopping us from considering other options. By encouraging us to think in a rigid all-or-nothing way, this leaves no room for anything else, including the possibility that it may not be true all of the time or even at all! When it becomes a habit and remains unnoticed, black-and-white thinking can leave us feeling hopeless and powerless to change anything.

Take Andi…

Andi has fallen into the habit of thinking about exam nerves in a black-and-white way. Words like 'always' and 'never' and 'can't' slip into Andi's black-and-white thoughts, making the thought seem like a fact and leaving little room for doubt.

> *Black-and-white thought*: 'I *always* get nervous and *can't* do anything about it, therefore exam nerves will *always* get the better of me, and I will *always* fail.'

> *Assumed fact*: Exams = uncontrollable nerves = failure.

This leaves no room for Andi to think about any occasions when exam nerves weren't *totally* uncontrollable. Although Andi feels overwhelmed with nerves at exam time, it is very unlikely that exam nerves are totally uncontrollable all of the time. However, by presenting this as an absolute truth, black-and-white thinking stops Andi from considering any occasions where exam nerves might not have been as overwhelming. It also stops Andi from thinking about what to do to control exam nerves better the next time. If Andi continues to believe unhelpful thoughts are facts rather than just thoughts, then Andi won't see the point in trying to respond to them differently.

> *Impact on life*: Uncontrollable nerves no matter what I do = fact = no point in trying to change it = I'm a failure = stop trying.

You know it's an unhelpful thinking habit when...

Here are some thoughts from the Workout Team about black-and-white thinking. You know it's an unhelpful thinking habit when...

> *...you usually give up on stuff because what difference will it make anyway?*

> *...you often use labels to describe yourself and others.*

> *...you don't really believe what other people tell you...they don't understand because they've got it so much easier than you.*

> *...sometimes you feel like there's no point in trying because that's just the way it is.*

…you often feel overwhelmed by things.

…you think that whatever you do is never good enough.

Left unchecked, black-and-white thinking can negatively affect your mental health and wellbeing. Constantly thinking in all-or-nothing terms or absolutes can leave you feeling that there's little point in trying to change things. It can also encourage you to compare yourself unfavourably to others who seem to manage things much better than you. In turn, these feelings can affect what you do, making you less able to think of solutions or the way to navigate through challenge, and making you doubt your ability to cope with lots of other things too. Feeling not-good-enough and helpless will probably make you feel switched off and less willing to take a risk and try new things.

Remember the fight, flight or freeze response from Chapter 1? Black-and-white thinking can be helpful when we need to make quick decisions about whether to stay and fight, run away or hide. The problem is that in modern-day life we are unlikely to encounter real threats to our lives on a daily basis, so making quick decisions when there is no real threat can be harmful. If we constantly make polarised, rigid decisions, we leave no room for other possibilities and are likely to make incorrect, ill-informed and even harmful choices. This could then impact negatively on how we feel and behave.

If Andi continues to think things like, 'I always get so nervous before my exams, I can't control my nerves, nothing ever works, I'll never do as well as I could… I'm useless', this is not going to help Andi prepare for the exams or get exam nerves under control. In fact, this thinking is likely to make Andi's exam nerves even worse, and leave Andi feeling increasingly:

Low, helpless, hopeless, anxious, angry, irritated…

And feeling this way will affect Andi's behaviour. Because Andi feels hopeless and helpless about exam nerves, Andi will probably become more anxious and worried about being nervous itself! If they expect to have uncontrollable nerves, this will also make it more likely to happen. Andi will look out for signs that this is true and be less likely to look out for times when exam nerves are more manageable or not there at all. Over time, Andi might find that worry and anxiety affect other things too, like sleeping and eating and doing the things Andi usually enjoys. Andi might even begin to feel physically unwell and try to find other ways to block out or control the worry. If Andi starts to rely on unhelpful ways of coping, like eating or drinking too much, or avoiding other stressful situations, this could create even more problems. Left unchecked and unnoticed, the black-and-white thinking frenemy will sap Andi's energy and mental strength, so they miss out on all of the good things in life.

Fitness test: Could black-and-white thinking be sapping your mental strength?

Be honest! Read through the following statements and think about them carefully. Perhaps talk them through with someone you trust.

1. Do you often find yourself thinking in opposites or all-or-nothing ways like…

   She's perfect… I'm hopeless.

   They're so clever… I'm so stupid.

   Everyone other than me is happy with life…my life is rubbish.

   Why are things always so difficult for me when everyone else has it so much easier?

2. Do you struggle to see anything in between?

3. How often do you find yourself:

   → Giving up easily when things get tough, because there's really no point?

   → Becoming annoyed, jealous or irritated with others who seem to have it so much easier than you?

   → Giving up when things don't exactly go to plan? For example, thinking that your diet is totally ruined if you've eaten two biscuits, and you might as well eat that cream cake, bar of chocolate and jumbo bag of crisps too?

→ Only noticing the extremes? For example, noticing when you or others are really happy, or really sad, but what about the in-between?

→ Labelling yourself and others? For example, I'm boring, he's fascinating, she's stunning, he's talented…

→ Thinking in words like should, must, always, never, useless, impossible, can't, terrible, etc.?

Most of us will be able to think of occasions where these things might feel familiar, but try to consider how many of these statements would ring true for you on a regular basis.

If you're not sure about it, that's okay. It's not always easy to notice thoughts that have become habits. Try to watch out for this kind of thinking over the next week. Try to catch it in action, or spend some time at the end of each day thinking back. What happened? What did you notice? How did you feel? How did you respond to things? Was black-and-white thinking around? Keep a note of any all-or-nothing thoughts by writing them down in your workout notes or on your phone.

If black-and-white thinking feels a bit too familiar, take a look at the **Think-ercises** below to add to your **Warming Up exercises** and **Stretch and Flex-ercises**.

Think-ercises

These Think-ercises can help you break the black-and-white thinking habit. But remember that it can take time and practice to change any kind of habit, and this applies to thinking habits too. So choose the Think-ercises that work for you and stick with them!

1. Look for the middle ground

Looking for the middle ground involves thinking about the possibilities between the extremes and introducing more options. But this isn't always easy to do. Having a middle ground can make us feel less sure about things, and being less certain can be unsettling.

On the other hand, having more options and being less restricted can also be a really helpful way to think about things.

- When you notice a black-and-white thought, try to look for the middle ground by:

  - ☑ Giving the middle ground an identity. What would you call it? How would you describe it? What would it look like? The more you practise looking for the middle ground, the easier you will find it.

  - ☑ Keeping a list of the black-and-white thinking words you use to describe yourself and others.

- Write down as many alternatives as you can think of, to describe the bits inbetween:

  - ☑ Challenge yourself to use as many alternatives as you can to add some colour to your black-and-white thinking over the next few days and weeks. How would you notice and describe the shades in between the extremes? For example, if you are exhausted, the shades might be: tired, sleepy, drowsy, shattered, droopy, burned out, out of gas, worn out, weary, off-peak; or if you are feeling stupid, the shades might be: mistaken, made an error, dull, slow, off-colour, tired, not thinking straight today, still learning, sluggish…

2. Notice the exceptions and uncover the evidence

- 'She's clever…I'm stupid': is this true all of the time, most of the time or some of the time? Where is your proof that this is true all of the time?

- Think of times when you have been clever/funny/confident, etc.…even just a little bit!

- If you struggle to think of examples, be your own best friend. What would a supportive friend or family member say to you?

3. Question the all-or-nothing label

- Ask yourself if people can be both things at the same time:

  - ☑ For example, can you be clever and still do something stupid?

  - ☑ Can you be loyal to your friends and still let them down?

  - ☑ Can you fail at something but still be successful?

4. Re-create and rate the black-and-white thought

- Notice your black-and-white thinking throughout the day and write the thoughts down.

- Now re-write the thoughts and re-create them, remembering, for example, to notice exceptions, look for the middle ground and 'add colour' to the original black-and-white thought.

- Now rate the thoughts. For example:

  - ☑ 'I'm so depressed today.' Yes, I'm really fed up and low today, but is it true to say I am depressed and the worst I could be? Well, I've got out of bed and come to school. I'm really fed up and low but that might also be because I didn't sleep well last night. So I'm probably a bit tired too. On a scale of 1–10 where 10 is the worst, I'm probably at a 7–8.

  - ☑ 'I hate all of my lessons this morning.' Is that a true fact? Do I hate all of them all of the time? I suppose science isn't too bad sometimes, especially when we do practical experiments. And I don't feel strongly either way about French, and Madame Woods can be a laugh sometimes. I suppose I don't hate them all of the time, even though none of them are my favourites. On a scale of 1–10 where 10 is the worst, I suppose lessons this morning are at 6.5.

Andi's Mental Health and Wellbeing Workout

Take Andi, after the workout.

Andi decided the black-and-white thinking was getting out of control. Andi chose a combination of **Stretch and Flex-ercises** and **Think-ercises** to add to the **Warming Up exercises**.

This is what Andi's workout looked like.

> **WARMING UP**
>
> • I will try to get to know my thinking habits so I can spot my unhelpful black-and-white thoughts before they take over. I will start by noticing my thoughts when I'm doing everyday things, like walking to school and brushing my teeth. I'll notice if my thoughts are about things that have happened in the past or if they're about things that might happen, and how this makes me feel. I'll also practise focusing my attention on what is happening around me instead of being dragged along by my thoughts.

Stretch and Flex-ercises

• I will try to *let my unhelpful thoughts come and go* and not beat myself up about them. I'll tell myself:

> I'm only thinking in black and white again. That's okay. We all do it sometimes. I must remember that just because my black-and-white thought is saying I'm hopeless, it doesn't mean that I am. I can hear the thought and don't have to believe it. I can write it down and keep it for later. It's just a thought. I can sit this one out and not get caught up in this thought.

> There's black-and-white thinking again. I'm going to *focus on my breathing* so I don't get caught up in it. I'm going to count in for four and out for four and notice where I feel my breath…in my nostrils, in my chest or in my stomach.

Think-ercises

I've been writing down my back and white thoughts all week and I've noticed that I often use the words 'totally', 'always', 'hopeless' and 'never' when I'm thinking about my exam nerves. I am going to try to *look for the middle ground* and use some different words, such as 'sometimes', 'good-enough', 'okay', 'partly', 'a bit' or 'occasionally'. I'm going to keep these words in the notes on my phone or in my workbook so I can look at them and remember to use them.

- I am going to notice black-and-white thinking and try to rate and re-create the thoughts *by remembering to ask myself*:

   ☑ Is it true that my nerves *always* get the better of me or has there been a time when they weren't so bad? Has there been a time when I have managed them differently, even just a little bit?

   ☑ Can I be nervous and still do okay?

   ☑ On a scale of 1–10, how bad are my nerves today? Is it true to say that they sometimes or often get the better of me?

   ☑ It's true that they sometimes get the better of me, but last month when I did my mocks I was nervous but still managed to finish all of my maths paper on time. I got a good pass for that paper so they didn't get the better of me then.

NEGATIVE FILTERING
(AKA LOOKING THROUGH GLOOMY GOGGLES)

What is negative filtering?

Negative filtering is like looking at the world though a dark and gloomy filter or lens, when anything positive is immediately dismissed or discounted and replaced with a negative way of looking at things.

Negative filtering is quite common – most of us put on our gloomy goggles from time to time! Occasionally it can even be a helpful thing to do! Noticing the negatives can motivate us not to make the same mistakes again and to do something different the next time. After all, we often learn from our mistakes!

BUT…it can be an unhelpful way of thinking when it becomes so distorted that it stops you from seeing things in a more balanced way, and blocks out any of the positives. When this happens, negative thinking can become a problem.

When negative filtering takes over, it stops us from seeing anything other than the tough stuff. It really is like looking through a dark and gloomy lens. And when this becomes a habit it can be as if you're stuck in a universe of negativity with no way to escape. It can be an extremely unpleasant and harmful way to view the world, causing big and difficult feelings like low mood, anxiety and hopelessness.

Take Abi…

Abi is a great athlete and has scored many goals in her time. She trains hard and always does the best she can on the day. But this time things didn't go to plan and she missed a crucial shot. Even though her coach was really pleased with the way she prepared for the game and the effort she put into it, Abi discounts all the positives. It's as if she can't hear them – all she can hear is her negative thoughts telling her that she's not good enough. She doesn't believe what her coach is telling her; she only believes her unhelpful thoughts. In other words, negative filtering is taking control of Abi.

Negative filtering thrives when we become obsessed with the smallest error or mistake. Everything else takes a back seat to the things that haven't worked out for us. It's as if any positive or good things have never happened. They're not as important as the one negative thing. The negatives steal all of the status!

You know it's an unhelpful thinking habit when...

Here are some thoughts from the Workout Team about negative filtering. You know it's an unhelpful thinking habit when…

…you're always on the lookout for the bad stuff, and sometimes it doesn't feel 'right' unless you've found it.

…you often feel that things are hopeless and out of reach.

…you only remember the bad things people say.

…even when things are okay, you put your own negative 'spin' on it.

…you obsess about the one bad thing, even if everything else was fine.

…you think people say things just to be nice or kind and they don't really mean it.

…you run through things in your mind over and over again, obsessing about what went wrong…or even searching for it!

Left unchecked, negative filtering can harm your mental health and well-being. Constantly thinking negative thoughts about yourself, the things that you've done, and ignoring or discounting all the positives, can leave you feeling negative about life in general. This constant negative viewing of the world can sap your strength and energy, leaving you feeling totally worn out and helpless. If nothing you do makes you feel good enough, what more can you do?

If Abi continues to think things like, 'She's only saying that to be kind', 'It doesn't matter that I've played well in the past', 'My best isn't good enough' and 'If I've made a mistake, then nothing else matters', this could make her feel:

Low, helpless, hopeless, angry, out of control…

Over time this will affect Abi's wellbeing. Sometimes things don't work out how we want them to. That's the way life is. Unhelpful negative filtering is dangerous because it hooks onto the bad stuff and blows it up. This stops us from thinking about how we can get through the tough stuff and still feel good about ourselves. Negative filtering thoughts slap on hurtful labels, while totally ignoring any positives, giving a very one-sided version of events. So instead of helping Abi to think about what she could do differently in her next game, negative filtering points the finger and tells her she is useless while at the same time discounting all of the good passes and goals she made. If Abi continues to listen to negative filtering thoughts, they will sap her of all her mental strength.

Fitness test: Could negative filtering be sapping your mental strength?

Read through the following statements and try to be as honest as you can. Perhaps talk them through with someone you trust.

1. Do you often find yourself thinking or saying things like:

Nothing I do is ever good enough.

I feel like such a fraud.

They're only saying that to make me feel better/to be nice/kind.

I'm useless/a failure/hopeless.

2. Do you find yourself:

→ Going over and over things searching for the negatives, even when things have gone well?

→ Worrying excessively about the things that have gone wrong or could have been better, no matter how small and insignificant they are?

→ Ignoring or disbelieving the positives, no matter how big they are?

→ Never feeling happy or satisfied with yourself or the things you do?

→ Comparing yourself negatively to your friends?

→ Feeling like there's nothing you can do to change things?

→ Finding it difficult to accept praise or compliments?

Don't worry if you've answered 'yes' to some of these statements. If we're honest, many of us will recognise these thoughts from time to time. But if they are very familiar to you, it could be that negative filtering is trying to take over.

If you're not sure about it, that's okay. As we now know it's not always easy to notice your thoughts. It takes some training! Try to watch out for this way of thinking over the next week. Try to catch the thoughts in action and spend some time at the end of each day thinking back. What happened? What did you notice? How did you feel? How did you respond to things? Was negative filtering around? Keep a note of any negative filtering thoughts by writing them down in your workout notes or on your phone.

If you think that negative filtering could be a problem, choose some **Warming Up exercises**, **Stretch and Flex-ercises** and **Think-ercises** to create your own personal workout.

Think-ercises

You might decide that you want to take control of negative filtering thoughts. These Think-ercises can help you do this if you practise them regularly.

1. Interrogate the negative filtering thought

- Try some of the following ideas to change the way you treat the unhelpful thought:

  - ☑ Keep your unhelpful thoughts close. Make a list of your negative filtering thoughts in one week so you can get to know them and keep them close. Write them in your workbook notes or on your phone.

  - ☑ Ask yourself, is this true always, most of the time, some of the time, rarely or never? What is your evidence?

  - ☑ Look at some of the labels in your negative filtering thoughts. What is the proof that the labels are true? Always? Sometimes? Rarely? Never?

  - ☑ What are the pros and cons of thinking this way? Think about how the negative viewing makes you feel, and behave. Does negative viewing have any benefits for you?

2. Try a new filter

- Try to change the filter by:

  - ☑ **Making a case for the opposition.** Play the opposition and argue a case against the negative filtering thought. For example, if a familiar thought is, 'I'm such a failure, I totally messed up that last exam question. Why did I do that? I'm such a loser', what would the opposition say to argue against this thought? Be creative. For example, the opposition might say, 'Everyone messes up from time to time. So you messed up one question. What about all of the other questions that you didn't mess up? You're not a failure. You can fail one question and still pass the exam. And besides…I'll bet you never make that same mistake again! You learn from your mistakes. You held it together for most of the exam and your revision paid off. Just because you slipped up on one of the questions doesn't make you a loser.'

☑ **Looking for the missing information.** Take one of your negative filtering thoughts and study it like a detective by looking for the missing evidence. Think about what else you would want to know about the situation, whether something like this has happened before and what happened, what else might have contributed to the situation, where the evidence is that the thought is totally correct, whether it could be partially correct, or not correct at all, and if you need a second opinion.

Negative filtering thoughts are great at highlighting the negatives but not so good at noticing and highlighting the positives. Look for the positives and make a note of them. Try not to make a judgement about if they are worthy or true (remember – negative filtering will encourage you to dismiss and disbelieve them). Just accept them and write them down. Try to look back at your positives from time to time or even say them out loud. Perhaps you could write yourself a *positive filtering* mantra the next time you notice your negative filtering thoughts creeping up on you.

Abi's Mental Health and Wellbeing Workout

Take Abi, after her workout.

Abi decided that negative filtering was getting out of control. She signed up to some **Warming Up exercises**, **Stretch and Flex-ercises** and **Think-ercises**.

This is what she chose for her workout.

WARMING UP

- I'm going to practise paying attention to my body and where I experience emotions. I am going to try and notice what happens to me when I feel different emotions…pleasant emotions as well as difficult ones. For example, whenever I am disappointed I usually feel sick and headachy. I'm going to try to learn how to tune into my body earlier and notice the signs that big feelings are growing.

Stretch and Flex-ercises

- *Practise flexible thinking.* Over the next week I will practise being more flexible in how I think and see things. When I am training I will try to stand in my coach's shoes and see things from her point of view.

- *Notice the negative thoughts…and let them come and go.* When I notice myself slipping into negative thinking, I will try to notice it and accept that sometimes I look for the negatives in things. I will tell myself, 'That's okay'. It doesn't mean that the thought is true or that I have to listen to it. I will tell myself, 'It's just a thought, I don't have to do anything with it, I can sit it out and wait for it to pass.' I will write the thought down when I notice it and leave it for later.

Think-ercises

- *Change the filter.* I will try and change the filter by making a case for the opposition. When I notice myself thinking, 'I'm so useless, I've let myself down', I will try to think about the argument against this thought. It might be, 'Perhaps I haven't done as well as I hoped, but there is no evidence that I've totally let myself down. I can be successful and score a goal, and make a mistake and miss a goal in the same match.'

- *Let the positives count.* I will write a list of all the positives and try not to respond to the negative thoughts that tell me they don't count. I will include the positive things that other people say to me, even if I don't always believe them. I can look at this list when I hear the negative filtering thoughts again.

PERFECTIONISM

(AKA UNREAL IDEAL)

What is perfectionism?

Lets be clear...there's absolutely nothing wrong in aiming high and wanting to do your best. In fact, there may be occasions when nothing but your very best will do – a final exam, a driving test, a job interview. So aiming for perfection can sometimes be a good thing, especially if it helps you to focus on your goals, spurs you on, and you feel excited and invigorated about the challenge.

BUT...it can become a problem when the need to be the very best becomes so great that it overshadows everything else, especially if anything less than perfect makes you feel bad about yourself. No one can be perfect all of the time. If you're human, then you'll make mistakes! And yes, it doesn't always feel good when things don't go your way or when you make an error. But that's part of life, and we often learn from our mistakes.

When perfectionism takes hold, distress and anxiety about not doing well enough take over, and fear of failure spirals out of control. Sometimes fear and anxiety at the thought of doing anything short of your very best can be so disabling that it actually prevents you from doing anything at all. When that happens, it can be less about striving for excellence and more about the fear of anything less than perfect.

Unhelpful perfectionist thinking acts as if it is driven by the desire for perfection, when in actual fact it is driven by an intense fear of failure. And that's a very different thing! In fact, the path to perfection can be a long one with lots of obstacles along the way. Take an athlete who has won a gold medal in a major championship. When they stand on the podium, gold medal hanging proudly around their neck, all we can see is their talent and success. But behind that success lies determination and self-belief to work through the tough times, learn from mistakes and keep sight of the end goal. What we don't see are the years of training and hard work, where the athlete has had to overcome injury and disappointing performances when they've fallen far short of their best. Not all athletes can win. And not all athletes will win all of the time. However, having the *aim* to be the best that they can possibly be motivates them to work through the times when they perform badly, to learn from their mistakes, and to not give up. They might appear to have achieved perfection in their winning moment, but perfectionism would have had no place in their preparation, because ironically, unhelpful perfectionist thoughts do nothing to help you achieve your best.

Perfectionist thinking fears failure so much that it can make you feel unable to take a risk and try new things in case you fall short of perfect. Worry and anxiety about not being good enough can affect your self-esteem and confidence. In some cases it can cause you to shut down and give up altogether.

Take Sam…

Sam wants to do the best she can – nothing wrong with that. But Sam worries about making a mistake because she thinks mistakes are a weakness and a sign that she is struggling. She bought an erasable pen in the hope that a perfectly presented piece of work would make others think that she is perfect all of the time. Little did she know that the ink disappears in heat! All of the time and effort she put into completing her assignment with the erasable pen, so she *looked as if* she never made a mistake, was for nothing. Her hard work disappeared along with the ink when it evaporated under the heat of the radiator.

Sam has become more focused on the perception of perfection and the fear of failure than doing the best she can. Her drive for perfection doesn't energise her to want to try new things, or to learn from her efforts and set new goals. Her drive for perfection is more about keeping up an image that she never makes a mistake. It's an unreal ideal. It has become such a habit for Sam that it has taken all joy away from the challenge of the task itself, and she is totally focused on the need for perfection to save face. It's an impossible way to live. We ALL make mistakes from time to time and there are times when good enough is actually…good enough!

You know it's an unhelpful thinking habit when...

Here are some thoughts from the Workout Team about perfectionism. You know it's an unhelpful thinking habit when…

> *…you're so afraid of getting things wrong or being seen as a failure that it's all you can think about.*

> *…you worry what others think of you and believe they'll think less of you if you don't do well.*

> *…you're quick to spot failures and shortcomings – your own and other people's!*

> *…sometimes you can't seem to get things done and homework or assignments take so long because you need them to be perfect.*

> *…you hate it when people say how well you have done or how smart you are. What if they find out you're just a fake?*

> *…if it's not perfect it doesn't count.*

If Sam continues to be driven by the need to be perfect in everything she does, she's likely to become more and more anxious and afraid of getting things wrong. Sometimes worry and anxiety can grow so big that they lead to procrastination – putting things off or not bothering at all. Sam is likely to become so fearful of appearing less than perfect that she will begin to opt out of things she might enjoy and learn from, all because she's frightened of what others might think. She will be overcome by big and difficult feelings like worry, anxiety, dissatisfaction and unhappiness. These feelings will then affect what she does and how she interacts with others around her. Left unchecked, perfectionist thinking will negatively affect her mental health and wellbeing.

Fitness test: Could perfectionism be sapping your mental strength?

Read through the following statements and try to be as honest as you can. Perhaps talk them through with someone you trust.

1. Do you often find yourself thinking or saying things like:

   All mistakes are a sign of failure.

   If I'm not the best then I'm nothing.

   If I mess up then everyone will think I'm a fake/a loser/useless…

   I need to be the best at everything all of the time.

   I can't lose.

   I can't take that risk.

   I can't do that because I might look stupid.

   Or do you catch yourself thinking all-or-nothing thoughts – you're either a winner or a loser, a success or a failure, and nothing in between? Is perfectionist thinking working hand in hand with black-and-white thinking?

2. Do you find yourself:

→ Worrying more and more about what other people think of you? Maybe it keeps you up at night?

→ Feeling you don't measure up to others' expectations?

→ Feeling bad about yourself and the things you do?

→ Wanting to please and impress other people all of the time?

→ Taking pleasure in others' failures – their failure makes you feel better about yourself?

→ Checking things or redoing things over and over again?

→ Finding it hard to laugh at yourself and any mistake?

→ Constantly searching for the things you did wrong rather than things you got right?

→ Sometime feeling it's better not to bother at all than to try and maybe end up making a fool of yourself?

Take a look at how many you've noted. Don't worry if you think some of these things from time to time. That's normal! But if you are aware of these thoughts taking up a lot of your thinking space, then perfectionism could be trying to take over. Is it worth stopping and thinking about this a bit more? Do you need to break up with perfectionism?

If you're not sure about it, that's okay. It's not always easy to notice your thoughts. It takes some practice! Try to watch out for this way of thinking over the next week. Keep a note of any perfectionist thoughts by writing them down in your workout notes or on your phone. You might also notice some other unhelpful thoughts working alongside perfectionism.

Think-ercises

Remember that Think-ercises can help you change or challenge the thought, but unhelpful thinking habits don't disappear overnight. So don't worry if you find perfectionism slipping into your thoughts. That's normal and it doesn't mean you've failed! In fact, if you're noticing perfectionist thinking, it's probably a sign that your exercises are helping you to become more aware of your thoughts. So keep on doing your Warming Up exercises and Stretch and Flex-ercises to get to know your perfectionist thoughts. And remember, sometimes just noticing the unhelpful thought is enough to stop it taking control. If you'd like to add some Think-ercises to your workout, take a look at the ideas below.

1. Interact with perfectionism differently

- Keep a note of these questions on your phone or in your work-book. If you notice perfectionist thinking taking over, try working through the questions. Ask yourself:

  ☑ Does it really matter? How much? Will it matter to other people as much as it matters to me? Will this still matter tomorrow? How about next week? Next year?

  ☑ What is the worst that could happen? Go wild…think of as many outcomes as you can, no matter how unlikely. How would you cope if the worst actually happened? Write down your coping plan.

  ☑ Has something like this happened to me before? Does it still matter as much to me now? How did I get through it?

  ☑ What does good enough look like? How perfect do I have to be on this occasion? Which tasks will I give 100% effort and which ones don't matter so much?

  Try to find a compromise.

2. Make up your own mantra

- Think of some phrases you can repeat when you spot per-fectionism creeping up on you:

    All I can ever do is my very best!

    Making a mistake does not mean I'm stupid or a failure; it means I'm human.

    There will always be some things I am good at immediately, some things that will take a little more time and effort, and some things that will be challenging no matter what I do. I can choose where I want to focus my energy.

    Remember the bigger picture. Soon this won't matter as much as it does this very minute.

    What else can you come up with?

3. Look for examples of 'good enough'

- Gather evidence from the people around you or in the media of times when they have done a 'good enough' rather than a 'perfect' job:

    ☑ What happened? Can you always tell the difference between 'perfect' and 'good enough'?

    ☑ Look for examples when people have made mistakes. What happened? How did they cope?

    ☑ How might making a mistake have helped them to learn? Would things have turned out differently if they hadn't made the mistake?

    ☑ Remind yourself that making some mistakes is one way of learning and doing better next time.

4. Cut yourself some slack

- Practise cutting back on some of the things you do that don't need to be absolutely perfect all of the time:

  - ☑ For example, doing a run in a slower time or handing in homework with some crossings out. What else can you think of?

  - ☑ Note what happens and how it makes you feel.

5. Ditch the unreal ideal

- Try to think about what is realistic, fair and do-able:

  - ☑ What is a realistic achievement for you, in the time and space you have? For example, if your homework is due in the next day, how can you do your best in the time you have?

  - ☑ Remind yourself that many things can affect what your 'best' looks like. For example, if you have a week or a month to complete your assignment, or if it is a subject you are already familiar with, then your 'best' will vary. Be realistic!

6. Set time limits

- Try to time limit some of the things you do:

  - ☑ For example, give yourself a set time to do your homework. When the time is up accept that it is finished.

  - ☑ Resist the temptation to go back and re-write or change your work; instead, do something you enjoy in the time you save. Go on – treat yourself!

7. Re-write your script

- Catch some of your unhelpful perfectionist thoughts and re-write them:

☑ Look out for words that exaggerate the situation. For example, 'I totally messed up that exam. I'm a complete failure.'

☑ Break the thoughts down and interrogate them. Is this really true? Is 'totally' an accurate word or is it misleading? Could it be re-written as, 'I may have messed up some of the questions and I probably haven't done as well as I hoped. If I've made some mistakes I'll need to think about what I can do differently next time.'

Sam's Mental Health and Wellbeing Workout

Take Sam, after her workout.

Sam decided that perfectionism was getting out of control. She chose some **Warming Up exercises**, **Stretch and Flex-ercises** and some **Think-ercises** for her personal workout.

WARMING UP

- I am going to practise being in the here and now, first thing when I wake up and last thing at night, by concentrating on my breathing and the different things I can feel and hear around me.

Stretch and Flex-ercises

- *Notice the perfectionist thought and let it come and go.* I will try to notice when I feel anxious or overwhelmed at the thought of not being perfect. I will try to notice the signals in my body, such as my heart racing faster or feelings of sickness. When I notice these things I will try to ride them out and not panic even more. I'll say to myself:

    It's because perfectionism is here again. But it won't stay here forever. It will pass. Ride it out.

    Then I will place my hands on my stomach and focus on my stomach rising and falling as I breathe in and out.

- *Practise thinking flexibly.* Each week I will try to expand my flexible thinking by trying to stand in someone else's shoes and see an argument or a disagreement from their point of view.

Think-ercises

- *Cut myself some slack.* When I use a pencil for my homework, I will only allow myself a certain number of rubbings out. I'll start with ten, notice when perfectionist thoughts appear and try to let them come and go and stick to my aim. Every week I will reduce the number of mistakes I am allowed to rub out. My long-term aim is to do my homework in pen and to accept any errors. I will use the time I save not doing my homework over and over again to start a new TV box set.

- *Look for examples around me.* I will look out for people who do a 'good enough' job or who sometimes make mistakes. I will watch what happens and how they get through it. I will especially look out for how making a mistake can help people to learn and do better next time.

PERSONALISATION
(AKA OVER-OWNING IT)

What is personalisation?

Personalisation is a bit like *over*-owning it, because it's when you think you're to blame for absolutely everything. And the word 'blame' is important because personalisation involves thinking you're totally responsible for all the bad stuff that happens, even when there's no logical reason to back this up.

It's normal to go over things from time to time, wondering about the part we played – and this can be a good thing. Taking responsibility and 'owning it' can help us to think more carefully about our behaviour and how to develop and keep positive relationships. Reflecting on the things we've said and done can help us make choices about what we might want to do the same or differently next time. Considering the part we play in situations can help us think and behave more flexibly and extend our problem-solving.

It's true that what we say and do often has an impact on others. We take on lots of different roles in life. Think for a moment about all the different roles you take on with different people around you…best friend, student, son or daughter, brother or sister, cousin, rival or enemy, employee… and how the different roles you have with people will influence them in different ways. But influence isn't control. And at the end of the day what someone else says or does is ultimately up to them. Not everything can be traced back to you!

Personalisation can become a problem when you get in the habit of blaming yourself when things go wrong while ignoring all of the other factors that could have played a part as well. When personalisation gets out of control it can leave you feeling responsible for everything that doesn't go to plan, and leaves no space to think about anything else that could have contributed to the situation or the things that are beyond your control. Remember that unhelpful thinking is really good at pointing out the negatives and ignoring the positives? Well personalisation is no different. Unhelpful personalisation is great at pointing out all the negative ways you could have influenced a situation, but not so good at spotting the positive ways.

Personalisation is good mates with some of the other unhelpful thinking habits too. Personalisation blinkers you from seeing any of the possible positives in a situation, and works alongside black-and-white thinking. And it also involves a lot of guessing what's going on in other people's minds and predicting the future, just like mind reading thoughts.

Take Aisha…

Aisha is wondering why Rob hasn't returned her text. Has she thought about all the different reasons why this might be, positive and negative? No, she's jumped straight to the conclusion that because he has received and read her messages, he has chosen not to reply. And that must be because she has done something to annoy him. It doesn't matter what. Unhelpful personalisation will be ready with a hundred reasons why she has annoyed him, because personalisation has taken control and is behaving like a fact, blocking out any other thoughts that could give a more balanced picture.

You know it's an unhelpful thinking habit when...

Here are some thoughts from the Workout Team about personalisation. You know it's an unhelpful thinking habit when...

> ...you pick apart everything that's happened, constantly going over and over the things you said and did.

> ...you feel guilty and worried most of the time...even when you don't know why.

> ...you feel like things are always your fault, even when you know deep down that it can't be.

> ...if someone says something, or something bad happens, you immediately think, 'What have I done...?'

Left unnoticed, personalisation can negatively affect your mental health and wellbeing. Constantly worrying about what you've said or done and carrying the blame on your shoulders can weigh you down, leaving you feeling worried, anxious and less able to focus on and enjoy the good things in your life. And these feelings can affect what you do, perhaps making you behave differently, such as not being yourself with your friends or avoiding them altogether.

If Aisha continues to think things like, 'It's all my fault' or 'What have I done?', this could make her feel:

Anxious, worried, guilty, hopeless, helpless...

And feeling this way could affect what Aisha does next. Imagine if Aisha decides she has annoyed Rob and he doesn't want to be mates with her any more. She stays out of his way and avoids him. But Rob hasn't texted her back because he was really sick last night. So the next day when Aisha avoids him he wonders what's happening, why is Aisha being so cold towards him? And Rob might think, 'Aisha hasn't bothered to ask how I'm feeling. Some friend she is…' and so the situation spirals out of control all thanks to unhelpful personalisation.

If Aisha gets into the habit of believing her unhelpful thoughts, over time it will sap Aisha's mental strength, leaving her feeling increasingly vulnerable, confused, anxious and agitated.

Fitness test: Could personalisation be sapping your mental strength?

Read through the following statements and try to be as honest as you can. Perhaps talk them through with someone you trust.

1. Do you often find yourself thinking or saying things like:

> *This is all my fault…*

> *I'm to blame…*

> *What have I done?*

> *Why me?*

> *It's so unfair…*

2. Do you find yourself:

→ Thinking that the bad stuff has always got something to do with you?

→ Feeling like you are carrying the world on your shoulders?

→ Feeling regularly overcome with feelings of guilt and worry?

→ Not taking the same responsibly for the good stuff?

Some of those statements might sound pretty familiar to us, and that's entirely normal. Remember that we have lots of thoughts passing through our minds all of the time. But if these statements feel a bit too familiar, and they're taking up a lot of space in your mind, then maybe personalisation could be trying to take control.

Don't worry if you're not sure. Thoughts can be so automatic that it's not always easy to notice them. Try to watch out for this way of thinking over the next week or so. Perhaps set aside some time each day to reflect on where your thoughts have taken you. Write them down and see if personalisation is hanging around.

If you decide you'd like to take back some control, then choose some **Warming Up exercises**, **Stretch and Flex-ercises** and **Think-ercises** to create your own personal workout.

Think-ercises

Here are some exercises to help you challenge and change personalisation thoughts. Take a look at them and choose the ones you'd like to add to your workout.

1. Balance your thinking

- *Do a personalisation pie chart.* Imagine a pie cut into six equal slices. Now think about the situation that's worrying you:

  ☑ How much was really your responsibility? One slice of the pie, two slices?

  ☑ What proof do you have? What would someone you trust say about the part you played? How big would they make your slice of the pie?

  ☑ What else could have had an influence on this situation?

  ☑ Do a personalisation pie chart to help you take a realistic look at blame.

- *Do a pros and cons list for thinking this way.* How does personalisation make you feel? Is this a pro or a con?

☑ Does personalisation help you to be realistic? Sometimes, always, never?

☑ What would you do differently if you didn't personalise this?

☑ Does personalising help you to think of different ways to respond, or does it restrict you?

☑ Remember to think about how personalisation affects your mood, thoughts and actions – would you feel differently or behave differently if you gave personalisation less space?

2. Problem-solve with your best friend

- *Talk to a good friend who you trust or be your own best friend!* Try not to respond to personalisation and listen to what a good friend would say to you about the situation:

   ☑ What would they encourage you to do? Who would they encourage you to talk to?

   ☑ What best friend advice would you give?

   ☑ Is there anything you could you do to help the situation right now?

   ☑ Be creative and think of as many other reasons for the situation as you can. Do this with a friend. See how many different possibilities you can come up with, no matter how bizarre!!

3. Remove the personalisation blinkers

- Try to look trough a positive lens and get in the habit of noticing the good stuff:

   ☑ Every day try to write down three things you are thankful for, no matter how small.

4. Look out for other unhelpful thinking habits

- What other unhelpful thoughts are working alongside personalisation? Mind reading? Negative filtering? Catastrophising? Any others? Noticing and acknowledging them can make them less powerful!

Aisha's Mental Health and Wellbeing Workout

Take Aisha, after her workout.

Aisha decided that personalisation was leaving no space for her other thoughts and she wanted to do something about it. She copied some **Warming Up exercises**, **Stretch and Flex-ercises** and **Think-ercises** in the notes on her phone so she would be more likely to have them at hand and stick to them. Here's what she wrote:

> ### WARMING UP
>
> * I am going to try and get to know my thoughts better by writing some of them down throughout the day, and noticing how they make me feel. I will try to notice some of my helpful, positive thoughts as well as the unhelpful ones.

Stretch and Flex-ercises

* *Practise flexible thinking.* I will try to think of as many different solutions to a problem as I can, no matter how strange they might sound. So if I am stressed because Rob hasn't texted or called me, I will try to think of as many different reasons why. I will write them all down, no matter how crazy they sound!

* *Notice and play around with the personalisation frenemy.* I know that when I try to stop thinking unhelpful thoughts, I obsess about them even more. When Rob didn't text me back I couldn't get rid of the thought that I had done something to upset him. Next time that happens I will try to make personalisation less important by playing around with the thought. When I notice the personalisation thought I will make a note of it on my phone and play around with it by reading it out loud in a French accent, or imagine it changing colour like a flashing Christmas tree light.

Think-ercises

When I notice I'm blaming myself for things that have happened, I will read this and try to:

- *Engage my problem-solving best friend.* I will remind myself I don't have to respond to the personalisation thought, and try to work with my problem-solving best friend instead. I'll build on some of my positive thoughts from the Warming Up exercises and will ask myself:

    ☑ Is there anything I can do to solve the problem right now? For example, could I ring Rob or send him a text?

    ☑ What might make me feel better right now?

    ☑ Is there anyone else who can help me think this through?

- *Take off the blinkers.* At the end of every day I will make a note of three things I am thankful for.

MIND READING
(AKA FILLING IN THE BLANKS)

What is mind reading?

Life can be complicated and other people can be confusing. We don't always understand why things happen or why people say and do the things they do. Sometimes we don't have all the information we need to make sense of others' actions or to make decisions about what to do next. So our thoughts try to fill in the blanks.

Sometimes trying to stand in other people's shoes and imagining how they might be feeling or the things they might be thinking can be a good thing. Trying to fill in the blanks can help us to understand other people and predict how they might behave. This can help us to change and adapt our behaviour too, so we can all get along better.

BUT…it's only helpful when we remember that we can't *really* see into other people's minds and therefore we can never *really* be certain what they are thinking or feeling. It's all guesswork. Sometimes we might get it right…and sometimes we will be way off the mark. And while it can be helpful to try and guess what motivates others, we need to keep an open mind to other possibilities too, and remember that we can never know for sure what is going on in someone else's thoughts.

Unhelpful mind reading thoughts act as if they know exactly what other people are feeling and thinking. And these thoughts are experts at jumping to negative conclusions about the reasons people say and do the things they do. Unhelpful mind reading thoughts cling to the negative and never ever come up with any positive possibilities. And like all unhelpful thinking habits, they present the thoughts as facts, closing the door on flexible thinking and problem-solving. So when mind reading convinces you of the worst, you act as if it's true.

Take Louis…

Louis is giving his class presentation, and although he doesn't really like public speaking, he thinks it is going okay, until he sees Mia yawning in the front row and mind reading thoughts jump in to tell him that Mia is yawning because he is boring. Louis listens to the unhelpful thoughts and believes them, so he begins to feel embarrassed and stupid and… well…boring. He can't see past Mia in the front row to all of the other students in the class, the ones who are nodding along with him, smiling, listening, taking notes. Louis starts to stutter and stumble over his words. He blushes. He wishes it was all over. His focus is entirely on Mia, who is yawning because he's boring. Didn't mind reading tell him so?

Because Louis takes the unhelpful thought as a fact, it affects his own feelings and behaviour in a negative way. But what he doesn't know is that Mia was out late last night with her new boyfriend. She stayed out far later than she should have and then had to listen to her parents go on and on at her when she eventually got home. And she was so wound up when she climbed into bed that she couldn't sleep. This morning she's understandably shattered. She's finding it hard to focus. All she wants is to crawl back into her warm bed…

Unhelpful mind reading has taken control. It hasn't allowed any space to consider the other reasons for Mia's yawns, and jumps straight to the conclusion that Louis is boring her. If Louis continues to listen unquestioningly to mind reading thoughts, he will get into the habit of thinking the worst. It will chip away at his confidence and self-belief. He'll begin to behave as if mind reading is telling him the absolute truth and won't question it or look for other explanations. And he will start to behave as if it is true too.

You know it's an unhelpful thinking habit when…

Here are some thoughts from the Workout Team about mind reading. You know it's an unhelpful thinking habit when…

…you're always trying to second-guess what others are thinking about you.

…you get stuck on things that have happened and play things over and over in your mind, on the lookout for signs to prove your beliefs about others are right.

…you quickly jump to conclusions about other people.

…what you imagine other people are thinking really gets under your skin, and changes your mood and affects your day.

…you think you're really sensitive and can pick up on others' feelings easily.

…it's the negative stuff that sticks. At the end of the day you find it hard to recall anything good.

…you get caught up in all the things you can't do or have messed up rather than the things you can do.

…you don't look for facts and rely on your instincts.

Unhelpful mind reading thoughts can creep up on you and take over, affecting how you feel about yourself and the people around you. Constantly believing these negative thoughts can make you feel low and not good enough. This can then affect what you do and how you behave with others.

If Louis continues to listen to mind reading thoughts like, 'Mia's yawning because she thinks I'm boring', 'I knew no one would be interested in my presentation' and 'I'm so bad at public speaking', this could make him feel a range of big and difficult feelings, including:

Anxious, inadequate, helpless, hopeless, angry, low, tired…

And these big and difficult feelings will affect his behaviour. For instance, Louis might:

→ Avoid presenting in front of his class again.

→ Avoid, challenge or ignore Mia because of his assumptions about her.

→ Hide away and feel ashamed.

→ Lash out and defend himself.

→ Worry even more about what others think of him.

Over time, mind reading will have a bigger and bigger impact. Louis' life and choices will be driven by his mind reading assumptions. Mind reading will be sapping his mental strength.

Fitness test: Could mind reading be sapping your mental strength?

We all mind read from time to time. It's part of human nature to try and work out other people. But unhelpful mind reading habits focus only on the negative. Could mind reading be getting out of control for you? Read through the following statements and see if they seem familiar. Perhaps talk them through with someone you trust if you're unsure.

1. Do you often try to second-guess what others are thinking and feeling? Do you find yourself thinking things like:

   She only said that because she's angry with me.

   He didn't respond to my invite/text/email because he doesn't want anything to do with me.

   She's laughing because she thinks I'm a loser.

   They ignored me because they don't want to hang out with me any more.

2. Are you constantly on the alert for the small signs that might indicate what people are thinking and feeling? Are you hyper-sensitive to things like facial expression, body posture, tone of voice, etc.? Do you find yourself looking for clues to explain what they are thinking, and do you always come up with the negative explanations?

   He always sits like that when he's mad.

   She's not smiling, so she must be upset.

   Magda's talking in her school teacher voice. She's annoyed with me.

3. Do you live your life based on negative mind reading assumptions? Is your behaviour influenced by negative mind reading?

> *He always sits like that when he's mad…so I'm going to keep away from him.*

> *She's not smiling; she must be upset…I'd better not say anything in case I make it worse.*

> *Magda's talking in her school teacher voice. She's annoyed with me. Who does she think she is? I'm going to tell her exactly what I think of her.*

4. Do you expect people to behave in certain a way, especially if they have done so in the past? Do you judge people based on their past behaviour? *If they've been angry in the past then they will be angry again…*

Don't worry if you recognise some of these statements in your everyday thoughts. We have so many thoughts passing through our minds that we're bound to have some mind reading ones from time to time. But if negative mind reading thoughts seem familiar to you, and they are having an impact on your behaviour, then maybe mind reading is trying to take over.

Don't worry if you're not sure. Thoughts can be so automatic that it can be difficult to recognise them. Try to look out for mind reading thoughts over the next few days. Perhaps make a note of some of the thoughts you spot?

Remember, being aware of your unhelpful thoughts can make them less powerful. Try to practise your different exercises every day so you can get to know them better. Perhaps you'd like to choose some **Think-ercises** to add to your **Warming Up exercises** and **Stretch and Flex-ercises**?

Think-ercises

These Think-ercises can help you respond differently to the thought over time, but it takes practice; always starts by noticing when the thought is there.

1. Do a fact check

- Write down the mind reading thought when you spot it:

  - ☑ Now do a fact check, remembering to check ALL of the facts. What has actually happened? What was actually said? Don't confuse the thought with the facts!

  - ☑ Try to see if any of the facts match the thought. What were your intentions? What were the other person's intentions, and how do you really know that for a fact?

  - ☑ Do the facts of the situation bear any resemblance to the imagined, mind reading thoughts?

2. Do a reality check

- Remind yourself that you have no control over what other people say and do:

  - ☑ Keep a note of the following statements and look at them regularly so you can remember them when you spot the mind reading thought: 'Some people will like me no matter what I do, some people will like me once they get to know me and some people *won't* like me no matter what I do. I will focus on the first two.'

  - ☑ Remember that you only have a real influence over the things *you* say and do. You can give your opinion; sometimes it will make a difference and sometimes it won't!

  - ☑ Try to notice situations where you have given your opinion and it has made a difference and when it hasn't.

Don't judge yourself…remind yourself that you are only ever responsible for your own actions.

3. Listen to lessons from the past

- Think about any similar situations that have happened before:

    ☑ Were there times when your mind reading thoughts were helpful and got it right? And were there times when the thoughts got it wrong?

    ☑ Remind yourself that mind reading thoughts usually jump to unhelpful negative conclusions.

    ☑ Think about the occasions when mind reading thoughts got things wrong in the past and how this affected the situation, your behaviour and your wellbeing.

    ☑ How did you get through difficult times with mind reading thoughts in the past? Remember that you have the ability to get through things even if the worst happens. Trust yourself that you will find ways to get through things again.

4. Treat the thought differently

- Acknowledge the thought and try to treat it kindly: 'Okay, I've heard you. Thanks for that, that's one possibility. I know you can get anxious about other people…let's wait and see. Let's sit it out until we know for sure.'

- Try agreeing with the thought and plan your next steps: 'Okay… so if that is true I can ignore it, talk to her about it, talk to someone else about it, wait and see if it happens again, never have anything to do with her again…'

- Try to think of as many options as you can.

- Play the opposition to the thought, and seek further evidence: 'We don't know that for sure. What proof do you have? Come back when you have evidence and know that for sure.'

Louis' Mental Health and Wellbeing Workout

Take Louis, after his workout.

Louis realised that mind reading thoughts were beginning to affect his life. He thought about the phrase 'Keep your enemies closer' and decided it could be a good thing to keep this unhelpful thought closer. Here's what his workout looked like.

WARMING UP

- I want to get better at staying calm and not panicking when I am feeling overwhelmed or anxious. I'm going to practise focusing on my breathing throughout the day. I'm going to set myself a reminder at different times so that I can focus on my breathing, and notice how I am feeling at different times in the day. If I can practise this, then I might be able to focus on my breath when I am feeling stressed out too!

Stretch and Flex-ercises

• I will practise being *kind to myself* when I notice mind reading thoughts, by remembering to tell myself that it's normal for me to jump to conclusions when I feel nervous and uncomfortable. For example, I hate presenting in front of the class so it is normal for me to try to second-guess what everyone is thinking about me, and to think negative thoughts. But I need to remember that I only think like this when I'm stressed! I will tell myself I have these thoughts because I am human and it doesn't mean I have to respond to them.

• I will keep mind reading thoughts close by *writing them down and rating them*. For example, yesterday, when I was presenting in class, the thought was very strong and at a 9/10. But today it's much less powerful, at a 5/10. Next week it will probably matter much less and drop to a 1 or a 2.

Think-ercises

• When I notice the unhelpful thought I will try to *check out the facts* by spending some time thinking about what has actually happened. For example, I saw Mia yawn, but I didn't hear her say anything about being bored, or know for sure that she was yawning because of me. The facts were that she yawned during my presentation and that is all. Mind reading filled in all the other gaps. In this case the facts did not match the thought.

- I will remember to think about *occasions in the past* when the mind reading thought has jumped to conclusions and consider if this was helpful or not. For example, listening to the mind reading thought on this occasion didn't help at all as it made me more anxious and nervous and affected my presentation. The mind reading thought got it wrong on this occasion as Mia was tired, not bored. I will try to remember that unhelpful mind reading habits cling to the negative and often get it wrong!

EMOTIONAL REASONING
(AKA FEELINGS RULE, OKAY!)

What is emotional reasoning?

Emotional reasoning happens when our feelings take over, and we become so caught up on the emotional rollercoaster that we believe if we *feel* it then it must be true. Sometimes feelings can become so big and overwhelming that we don't stop to look at the facts or question anything else, including the unhelpful thoughts that underpin them. So we trust our feelings and go along with the negative thinking that always provides an unhelpful story to confirm the emotion.

For example:

I feel so guilty…therefore it's my fault and I must be to blame.

I feel so embarrassed…I must have looked really stupid.

There's nothing wrong in being in touch with your feelings and emotions. In fact, it can be really helpful to be emotionally aware. Our emotional response to situations can help prepare us for what we need to do next. For example, if we feel uneasy or afraid when we hear footsteps behind us in a dark street at night, this is a natural response to a possible threat. We will be more alert and vigilant, and we will look out for any other signs that indicate we might be in danger so that we can get out of the threatening situation.

BUT…when our emotions take over, we become less able to look out for other signs and signals. Our big feelings dictate and get in the way of logical thinking and problem-solving. When we're caught up in emotions, we're less able to direct out attention to other things. So we won't be able to concentrate or think things through. When this happens, emotional reasoning often gives us reasons to confirm and validate our big feelings, and blocks out everything else.

Take Alec…

Alec feels jealous when his boyfriend goes to band practice and talks about what a great time he has. Alec feels left out and worried that his boyfriend enjoys being with his band mates more than him. Feeling jealous is a normal human reaction and we all can feel jealous from time to time. The problem is that Alec discounts everything else and believes that his feelings of jealousy tell the whole story. When he feels jealous, the emotional reasoning thought fills in the gaps and tells Alec that he's jealous because his boyfriend is cheating on him. Unhelpful emotional reasoning takes over and leaves no room for any other explanations for his feelings of jealousy. This only makes the emotion stronger. And it's become such a habit for Alec that he doesn't question his thoughts or his feelings. Just because he feels it, he thinks it is true. Emotional reasoning is quick to provide a negative story to confirm his feelings. Alec is letting his 'feelings rule, okay!'

You know it's an unhelpful thinking habit when...

Here are some thoughts from the Workout Team about emotional reasoning. You know it's an unhelpful thinking habit when…

> …it makes no difference what other people say; you feel so emotional that you believe they're lying or just saying things to make you feel better.

> …you feel guilty about stuff and always think that things are your fault. For example, if you go into a shop and the assistant stares at you or follows you, you feel so guilty that you begin to think you've done something wrong!

> …sometimes you wake up in a mood and feel so angry that you act as if other people have done something to annoy you. You take your feelings out on them.

> …when you feel alone you really believe that no one cares about you at all.

Left unchecked, emotional reasoning can really affect your mental health. When you get into the habit of responding to your feelings without questioning the thoughts that lie behind them, they can become much bigger and overwhelming. And when emotional reasoning steps in to tell you why you feel that way, it doesn't allow you to think flexibly about other possibilities. So you become fixated on the reasons that confirm your feelings without thinking about anything else. And emotional reasoning is an expert at focusing in on all the negative, worst possible scenario explanations for your feelings. This can leave you feeling increasingly hopeless, unworthy, anxious, angry and fearful.

If Alec continues to think things like, 'I feel jealous, because he likes being with them more then me. If I feel jealous then he must be cheating', this could make him feel:

Angry, helpless, hopeless, low, unworthy…

And feeling this way could affect what he does. For example, if emotional reasoning thoughts convince Alec that his boyfriend is cheating, he might begin to behave differently towards him. He might accuse him, argue with him, trust him less, push him away…

And if emotional reasoning has got it wrong and his boyfriend isn't cheating, then this could really affect their relationship and how Alec trusts others and behaves in other relationships too. Emotional reasoning could sap all of his mental strength.

Fitness test: Could emotional reasoning be sapping your mental strength?

Read through the following statements and try to be as honest as you can. Perhaps talk them through with someone you trust.

1. Do you often find yourself noticing your emotions and jumping to conclusions about them? For example:

   I feel worried and I'm sure something's happened to her/him…

   I am scared because this is really frightening…

   I feel ashamed so I'm to blame…

   I feel so stupid because I'm no good at this…

2. Do you often feel or behave in the following ways?

→ Experiencing sudden big feelings without any build-up, as if you are completely hijacked by your emotions?

→ Saying or doing things you regret later because of how you felt at the time?

→ Feeling worthless and not good enough?

→ Putting things off because you feel so bad about them, and what's the point anyway (sometimes known as procrastinating)?

Don't worry if you answered 'yes' to a few of those statements. That's entirely normal. But perhaps you think or feel this way quite often, and you don't want to let it get out of control?

But if you're not really sure about it, that's okay too. It's not always easy to notice your thoughts. It takes some practice! Try to watch out for this way of thinking over the next week.

Try to catch emotional reasoning in action, or spend some time at the end of each day thinking back. What happened? What did you notice? How did you feel? How did you respond to things? Was emotional reasoning around? Keep a note of times when thoughts have jumped to conclusions or filled in the gaps about your emotions. Jot them down in your workout notes or on your phone.

If you would like to keep emotional reasoning under control, try out some **Warming Up exercises**, **Stretch and Flex-ercises** and **Think-ercises** to make your personal workout.

Think-ercises

Take a look at these Think-ercises and see if they could help you change the shape of emotional reasoning.

1. Separate the feelings from the facts

• When you notice emotional reasoning, try to separate the thoughts and feelings from the facts:

☑ For example, if you feel angry, emotional reasoning might tell you, 'You feel angry so they must have been mean to you.' Try to separate the thought and feeling from the fact by looking around you for evidence. Can you actually see or hear anything that would prove that someone is being mean to you? Can you see or hear anything that gives a different perspective and proves the thought is not a fact?

☑ Now decide whether your initial emotion was a good guide to what was happening, or did emotional reasoning fill in the gaps too quickly? For example, did your angry feelings really prove that others were being mean, or could those feelings be due to something else? Did emotional reasoning jump to conclusions?

2. Put on your chill-out specs

- Try to notice when you are looking through an emotional lens and remember to put on your chill-out specs:

☑ Try to notice the emotion in your body. Where do you feel big emotions like anger, worry, stress, sadness, fear? Do you feel the emotion in your stomach? Does it clench, give you butterflies or make you feel sick? Or do you feel it elsewhere…do you feel hot, clammy, cold? Do you tense up? Do you feel shaky? Do you get a headache? Something else? Try to notice where you feel emotions in your body.

☑ Try to wait for your emotions to pass or lessen. Big feelings can't last forever. Try to focus on your breath and try some of your Stretch and Flex-ercises to keep you in the moment while your initial emotions become less powerful.

☑ Now think about how you might respond if your emotions didn't take over. Would this change how you thought about the situation?

3. Become a problem-solver

- What if you agreed with the emotional reasoning thought, as if it was correct or partly correct? What could you do? Think of as many different things as you can to help you get through the situation. Be creative!

4. Be your own best friend

- Imagine your best friend was having exactly the same thoughts and feelings as you:

  ☑ What would you say to them?

  ☑ What advice would you give?

  ☑ Now be your own best friend and take your own advice!

Alec's Mental Health and Wellbeing Workout

Take Alec, after his workout.

Alec wanted to get to know his emotional reasoning thoughts better. He chose a combination of **Warming Up exercises**, **Stretch and Flex-ercises** and **Think-ercises**. Here's what his workout looked like.

WARMING UP

- Sometimes I don't realise that emotional reasoning thoughts have taken over and I am caught up in bad feelings before I know it. I will practise *staying in the here and now* so that I can get better at noticing my thoughts and feelings sooner. I will try to spend at least 5 minutes every day noticing the here and now by noticing the sounds around me, the feeling and sensations of my body where I am sitting, and noticing my breathing. I will look out for:

- 5 things I can see.

- 4 things I can hear.

- 3 things I can touch.

- 2 things I can smell.

- 1 thing you can taste.

Stretch and Flex-ercises

- When I notice the unhelpful emotional reasoning thought I will try to accept it and wait for it to pass. For example, I often feel jealous when I think that my boyfriend has more fun at band practice than with me. Jealousy is a normal feeling and my thoughts will often try to fill in the gaps. But I don't have to respond or do anything with them. The feeling won't last forever and nor will the thought…they will pass.

Think-ercises

- I will try to change my lens and put on my *chill-out specs* by noticing where I feel my emotions in my body. I will keep a note of where in my body I feel big and difficult emotions like jealousy. I will try to notice where they start and how they grow. I will try to separate my feelings from the facts and what I would think about the situation if my big feelings weren't as powerful. How would

I behave differently if the emotional reasoning thought was less powerful?

- I will also try to separate my thoughts and feelings from the facts by looking around for evidence. I will look out for the things I can hear or see that give a different perspective on the situation, then consider if the initial feeling was helpful or if emotional reasoning jumped too quickly to fill in the gaps.

LIVING THE LIFE YOU WANT TO LEAD...

Now you have read (or flicked) through this book, I wonder what you are thinking now?

My mental health is important and I can look after it, just like my physical health!

Unhelpful thoughts are really good at pointing out the negatives and shouting you down... but they're just thoughts. Not facts.

Everyone will have unhelpful thoughts from time to time... so I don't have to feel bad about it. It's all part of being human!

I don't have to do anything with unhelpful thoughts...but if I notice them, then I can choose what I want to do next.

Stretch and Flex-ercises can help me get to know my unhelpful thoughts and keep them close.

Adding some Think-ercises to my workout can help me respond differently to unhelpful thoughts.

Being a teenager or young person is intense. It can be challenging, exciting, frightening, confusing, and a whole lot more. It's a time of change and uncertainty…fluctuating hormones and a developing body, new relationships, and unanswered questions about who you will become, who you will love and what you will do next. Add to that the challenges of modern-day life – exams, peer pressure, family, finances, world events and global uncertainty, to name only a few! And in today's world teenagers don't only have to worry about the opinions of people around them, but also what the world of social media thinks as well. The complications of juggling a social media identity – how you present yourself online, stay connected and handle your online relationships – can all add to the intensity. Therefore getting into good habits for your mental fitness has never been more important.

There are lots of things that can help your mental wellbeing, and becoming aware of your unhelpful thinking habits, or frenemy thoughts, is one of them. It's important not to let unhelpful thoughts take up all of your thinking space, and to keep plenty of room for the things that matter most to you.

So let's think about what really matters to you and how you can keep sight of these things, even through the inevitable tough times.

Living YOUR life YOUR way…

Unhelpful thinking habits are good at shrinking your world by pointing out the negatives and focusing on the things that could go wrong. But remember, just because things might go wrong it doesn't mean that they will! The rigid messages that unhelpful thoughts give can restrict the things that you do and try because they constantly chip away at your confidence and self-belief. Being constantly bombarded by unhelpful thoughts can be exhausting and leave you feeling in a really bad place and unable to cope with anything.

Don't let unhelpful thinking habits shrink your world and the things you want to do. It's important to live the life you want to lead without being led by unhelpful thinking.

As well as practising the exercises in your Mental Health and Wellbeing Workout, try to counteract unhelpful thoughts by spending some time recognising your own unique strengths and the things that matter most to you in your life. Let's think about these things right now.

A good place to start is to think of what you enjoy and choose to do. What do you naturally gravitate towards?

Think about it…

What matters most to you?

How would you respond to the following:

→ What things do you enjoy most in life? What makes you feel content? What makes you laugh? What makes you happy?

→ What is important to you? Name your top three things.

→ What do you value most in your life? Think of the people, activities, experiences, hopes and opportunities that matter most to you.

→ What do you need in your life to make all of the above happen?

If you don't immediately know, don't worry! We don't always stop to think about the things that matter most, as we can be hijacked by other thoughts. Try considering the following:

→ When you've had a good day, what has made it good?

→ If you could plan your perfect week, what would it include?

→ Think of your happy place. Where would that be? Who would be there? What would you be doing?

➜ What things are important to you right now? What things are important to you over the next week, month, year?

Make a note of your ideas.

What are your unique strengths?

Now let's think about your own unique combination of strengths. Unhelpful thoughts focus on the negatives, the mistakes you make and the things that you might not have done as well as you wanted. Spending time thinking about what you do well and your strengths is important for more balanced thinking. Chances are you're drawing on your strengths when you're doing many of the things you enjoy.

However, thinking about strengths doesn't only have to be about your success and the things you do well; it's also helpful to think about the things you do that fill you with energy, enthusiasm and happiness. Your strengths are the things that make you feel alive! It's possible that the things you are good at are the same as the things that make you happy and energised. But they don't have to be.

Here are some ideas adapted from a list of well-known strengths and virtues by Christopher Peterson and Martin Seligman (2004).[1] They suggest that being able to identify and use your own strengths is important for mental health and wellbeing, and that we are at our happiest when we use our personal, or signature strengths. Have a read through the list on the next page and see which signature strengths you recognise in yourself. You might even want to add some of your own!

Remember, no strength is better or worse than another, and strengths can change over time according to what is happening in your life. While we are all likely to have aspects of different strengths, some of them will probably feel more familiar to you than others. That's because we all have our own unique set of strengths and abilities that make us who we are. Being aware of our strengths can help us focus on the things we can do to make the most them, as well as building on those we want to develop,

---

1 Peterson, C. and Seligman, M. (2004) *Character Strengths and Virtues: A Handbook and Classification.* Oxford: Oxford University Press.

and recognising and drawing on the strengths of people around us when we need to. Connecting with your strengths can help you feel energised, fulfilled and motivated – and that's good news for your mental health!

So when you look at the list below, try to focus on how you *feel* when you draw on each strength. For example, the first strength is about a love of learning. Some of you may be very successful and talented learners, but learning new things may not necessarily make you feel happy and invigorated. This means that other character strengths may be more important to you. So it's not about having strengths in the sense of possessing talents and skills, but more about which strengths make you feel alive, invigorated and at your best. Have a read through and see which ones you identify with. Do you identify more strongly with some of them?

When do you thrive? (aka What gives you a buzz?)

1. Are you a lover of learning?

Forget about how much you know or how clever you think you are, and let's focus instead on the pleasure you get from learning new things and how you use your new knowledge:

- Are you someone who enjoys trying new things and often tries to problem-solve in lots of different ways?

- Are you happiest when you're discovering or doing something new?

- Do you like to think things through to consider the most effective way of doing things?

- How do you feel when you're discovering new things and problem-solving? Does it make you feel energised, excited, happy, satisfied…?

- Do you feel at your best when you're learning new things and filled with curiosity?

Don't worry if this doesn't sound like you…it doesn't mean that you're not good a good learner…it just means that this isn't what invigorates you or makes you feel at your best.

2. Do you have focus and a desire to see things through?

How do you feel when you're faced with a challenge or problem? How happy are you when you need to be strong and stand up for what you believe in, or stick with something right through to the end, no matter how difficult it is. Remember, it's not about how well you do this, but about how satisfied and content it makes you feel:

- How determined are you to see things through to the end, and to keep on going when the going gets tough – and do you enjoy it?

- Do you love a challenge and see obstacles as something to be worked through?

- Do you feel alive and invigorated when you are tackling things?

- Do you have the courage to stick to what you believe in, no matter what the consequences?

- Do you have a love for life, no matter what stands in your way?

- Do you enjoy getting stuff done?

- Are you always honest, even if your honesty isn't welcome or accepted by others?

3. Are you a people person?

Let's think about the pleasure you get from being around other people, and supporting them. Although we all interact with others daily, concentrate on how this makes you feel, and if interacting with others energises you and helps you feel good about yourself:

- Do you thrive when you're around others – interacting, helping and connecting with people?

- Do you seem to 'get' other people and fit in effortlessly?

- Do you value being around other people and being able to support them in lots of different ways?

- Does being around others re-energise you and make you 'feel alive'?

- Do you like to socialise in your free time and do you find this relaxing? Do you prefer to spend time with others rather than being alone?

- Do you find it easy to get on with most people, even if they are really different to you?

4. Is being a fair leader important to you?

Does the idea of leading others fill you with dread or excitement? Are you more comfortable taking a lead and directing others, or is that your worst nightmare? Let's think about how your sense of right and wrong guides what you do, and whether using your moral compass to lead others is something that you enjoy:

- Do you like to take the lead and are you driven by a strong sense of right and wrong?

- Are you able to encourage everyone to work together – and is this something that makes you feel satisfied and happy?

- Are you good at recognising and valuing others' individual strengths and skills?

- Are you at your best when you are able to support and organise others to get things done?

- Do you love helping others to work together as a team?

- Is treating everyone fairly important to you, and do you stick up for those who have been treated unjustly?

- Do you like to give everyone a chance?

5. Do you like to stand in other people's shoes?

Do you take pleasure in being able to see things from other perspectives and points of view, and does this come easily to you? Let's think about how important this is to you, and the satisfaction you take from being able to stand back, look at the facts and take a considered view:

- Do you like to stand in someone else's shoes and consider things from different points of view before responding?

- Are you often careful and cautious about the things you say and do?

- Are you most comfortable when you have the time to think things through?

- Are you the kind of person who doesn't hold a grudge?

- Are you able to understand why others might do the things they do, and are therefore able to forgive people more easily?

- Are you happiest when you're not in the limelight or the centre of attention?

- Do you believe that everyone's opinion is important and does this guide the things you do?

- Are you happiest when you can look at the pros and cons of a situation?

6. Do you like to look on the bright side?

Being excited by life and seeing possibilities rather than problems can be a helpful way to look at life, and it might come quite naturally to some of us. Perhaps you're a 'glass half full' kind of person and are at your best when you draw on the positives, and are able to help others to do this too?

- Are you the kind of person who loves to notice and appreciate the things you have around you...the people, places, experiences, opportunities?

- Do you find it easy to be grateful for the things you have rather than the things you don't?

- Do you also enjoy making others happy?

- Are you the one who tries to look on the bright side when you're with friends? Do you point out the good stuff, possibilities and things to look forward to?

- Do you use humour to cheer up yourself and others? Do you like nothing better than a good laugh?

- Is it important to you to remain hopeful and believe that everything will be okay in the end? Does this make you happy?

Read through the ideas to think about your own personal combination of strengths. When do you thrive? Perhaps talk to people who know you well and ask them to pick your top strengths. Sometimes other people might see different things in you. You might be surprised. But remember – you know yourself better than most!

Now take a look at the notes you made earlier about the things that matter to you. Which strengths are you drawing on when you do these things? Do the things you enjoy link in with your identified strengths? Do they match up or are they different? Remember to not get too hung up on skills and how well you do things or perform tasks. It's more about how you feel when you draw on your strengths.

Now think about the things you might want to do more of to make the most of your top strengths. Often when we are doing the things that make us happy and content, we're drawing on our natural strengths and virtues. What things are you going to make time for?

Are there any strengths you'd like to build on? Can you think of any activities you can do to develop these strengths? What might you want to do more of to support some of your other strengths?

Now let's get focused! What are you going to do to live the life you want to lead? What things are you going to try to do every day, every week, every month and every year that make the most of your unique strengths? How will you do this? Who do you need around you to help you make the most of your strengths and to help you do the things that matter most to you? How will you make space for the things that matter in your life?

Here are some of the things members of the Workout Team noted:

What matters most to me?

Spending time with my friends. When I imagine myself at my happiest I nearly always have my friends around me.

Having a laugh. I love to have a laugh and just be myself, without worrying about what others think of me. I can do this with my very best friends.

Looking after my dogs, walking them and spending time playing with them.

Having something to aim for, like saving up to go to a music festival or running charity races. I like to have something I am working towards.

What are my unique strengths?

I think I am the kind of person who is good with other people. I like being with my friends best of all and they all say that I am the one who keeps the group together. I think I am probably very much a people person as I feel at my best and happiest when I am around others and able to help them.

I also think I am the kind of person who looks on the bright side. When I am doing some of the things that matter most to me, like being with my friends, I like to make them laugh and feel good about themselves. This makes me feel good too. I get along with most people but I like to be the one my best friends turn to.

I've realised that it's also important for me to have a goal and to be working towards something. Other people probably don't know this about me but I love to have an aim and when I don't have one sometimes I can feel a bit lost. I think I am probably the kind of person who likes to see things through so I will try to be more aware of this and remember that I'm happy when I've got something to aim for. Maybe I need to think about how I can do this a bit more.

I'm going to try to set myself some short-term and long-term goals. I want to go on holiday with my friends next year to Spain so that is a good long-term goal to work towards. I'm going to try and get a part time job at the weekend so that I can save up for the holiday. A short-term goal is to go for a run three times a week as I'd like to do another 5km charity run in the summer.

I know I'm content and happy when I spend time with my friends, so I'm going to make sure I have planned time to spend with them every month. Then I'm not relying on it just 'happening'. We are going to have film nights twice a month at our houses where we all get together for a night in, watching our favourite films and eating our favourite food. We are going to make sure we do this even when we are busy with course work and exams!

Final thoughts

Changing your relationship with unhelpful thoughts is important for mental fitness. Whether that means becoming more aware of the thoughts and keeping them close so that they're not such a big deal, or responding to the thoughts in a different way, the key is finding what works best for you and committing to it.

And it's well worth the effort that this might take.

It takes some practice to break old habits, like listening to and believing unhelpful thoughts unquestioningly, and it can take some time to establish a new habit, like noticing, accepting and responding to the thoughts differently. Remembering your personal strengths and finding space for them in the everyday things you do can stop unhelpful thoughts taking up too much space in your life. And after all, you deserve to live your life your way…not the frenemy way! So go on, take your own steps with some final best friend truths to inspire you!

Don't let unhelpful thinking habits dictate who you are…be your own person.

Train your mind like a muscle – the stronger your mind, the more you can handle.

Don't look at the world through a negative lens – this only makes your world look smaller.

Can you remember who you were, before the frenemy told you who you should be?

Change starts in your thoughts. Don't believe everything you think.

The end.

INDEX

Also published by Jessica Kingsley Publishers

You Can Change the World!

Everyday Teen Heroes Who Dare to Make a Difference

ISBN 978 1 78592 502 3

My Anxiety Handbook

Getting Back on Track

ISBN 978 1 78592 440 8

Starving the Anxiety Gremlin

A Cognitive Behavioural Therapy Workbook on Anxiety Management for Young People

ISBN 978 1 84905 341 9

Banish Your Body Image Thief

A Cognitive Behavioural Therapy Workbook on Building Positive Body Image for Young People

ISBN 978 1 84905 463 8